When the Bough Breaks

The Pursuit of Motherhood

BY ALI SANDERS

We are proud to introduce The**inspirational**series™. Part of the Trigger family of innovative mental health books, The**inspirational**series™ tells the stories of the people who have battled and beaten mental health issues. For more information visit: www.triggerpublishing.com

THE AUTHOR

Ali Sanders is an author, school librarian, and mental health ambassador from Staffordshire. She has been writing since she first learned to hold a pencil and holds a BA (hons) in Creative Writing from the University of Derby. As well as writing about her experiences with pre- and postnatal mental health issues, Ali enjoys writing fiction, particularly short stories and poetry, and is currently planning her first full-length novel.

Outside of writing, Ali loves reading, long walks, good food, good wine, and listening to The Rolling Stones on repeat. She enjoys spending time with her husband, their young son, and their Devon Rex cat.

Ali credits her close-knit family and friends with helping her to deal with her anxiety, chronic insomnia and OCD. She aims to give a voice to anyone who is suffering because of perinatal mental health stigma, whether that be the women themselves, or their loved ones.

First published in Great Britain 2019 by Trigger

Trigger is a trading style of Shaw Callaghan Ltd & Shaw Callaghan 23 USA, INC.

The Foundation Centre

Navigation House, 48 Millgate, Newark

Nottinghamshire NG24 4TS UK

www.triggerpublishing.com

British Library Cataloguing in Publication Data

A CIP catalogue record for this book is available upon request from the British Library

ISBN: 978-1-78956-011-4

This book is also available in the following e-Book and Audio formats:

MOBI: 978-1-78956-014-5

EPUB: 978-1-78956-012-1

Cover design and typeset by Fusion Graphic Design Ltd

Printed and bound in Great Britain by Clays Ltd, Elcograf S.p.A

Paper from responsible sources

www.triggerpublishing.com

Thank you for purchasing this book.
You are making an incredible difference.

Proceeds from all Trigger books go directly to The Shaw Mind Foundation, a global charity that focuses entirely on mental health. To find out more about The Shaw Mind Foundation visit,
www.shawmindfoundation.org

MISSION STATEMENT

Our goal is to make help and support available for every single person in society, from all walks of life. We will never stop offering hope. These are our promises.

Trigger and The Shaw Mind Foundation

A NOTE FROM THE SERIES EDITOR

The Inspirational range from Trigger brings you genuine stories about our authors' experiences with mental health problems.

Some of the stories in our Inspirational range will move you to tears. Some will make you laugh. Some will make you feel angry, or surprised, or uplifted. Hopefully they will all change the way you see mental health problems.

These are stories we can all relate to and engage with. Stories of people experiencing mental health difficulties and finding their own ways to overcome them with dignity, humour, perseverance and spirit.

The desire for motherhood is something that many women experience, and for some it can be a struggle to get there. Ali was one of them.

Her journey will be heartachingly familiar to some, and new to others, but everyone can take something away from her fight to become a mother. Ali speaks up about issues that we often keep to ourselves, including depression and OCD, and shows through her story that dreams can be achieved despite these problems.

This is our Inspirational range. These are our stories. We hope you enjoy them. And most of all, we hope that they will educate and inspire you. That's what this range is all about.

Lauren Callaghan,
Co-founder and Lead Consultant Psychologist at Trigger

For 'The Girls', for keeping me laughing even when I thought there was no laughter left.

For Mum, Dad and Lizzie, for always being there to catch me when I started to fall.

For Michael, for sticking with me and refusing to stop loving me even when I made it difficult.

For the twins. I will never forget you and I promise to always put your gingerbread men on the Christmas tree.

Most of all, this book is for you, Jacob.
I love you all the way to the moon and back, and more than all the twinkly stars in all the twinkly sky.

Disclaimer: Some names and identifying details have been changed to protect the privacy of individuals.

Trigger Warning: This book contains references to suicidal thoughts.

INTRODUCTION

My two-year-old son, Jacob, is in his cot upstairs. He's not asleep yet; I can hear him kicking away and jabbering to himself on the baby monitor as I write this. My husband, Michael, has gone to watch a darts match with his friend and I'm here at home, relaxing on the sofa and writing.

Writing.

It seems incredible. This scene is something that, not so long ago, I thought would never be a reality for me again. For several reasons.

I've been a voracious writer since I was a child, when I'd interview an assortment of family members for my monthly "magazines" and then insist they buy a copy. I soon progressed to short stories and poetry. I even enjoyed writing essays and coursework at school – the more detailed I could make my work and the more research I had to do, the happier I was. So, you see, it seemed a natural progression for me to go on to study creative writing at degree level. I had never foreseen a time in my life that I wouldn't write, could never have imagined not wanting to. It was just a part of me, as inherent as eating or sleeping.

Sleeping. The word makes me shudder slightly. It's the one word that can, even to this day, cause waves of anxiety to sweep over me in an instant.

As for my reasons for thinking I'd never write again? To begin with, the thought of being able to relax enough to write (or indeed, to do anything that would give me pleasure) became alien to me for quite a significant period between 2015 and 2017, due to some quite complex mental health issues. For much of this time, I was on a constant state of high alert, completely wired and listening out for the faintest sound that Jacob made. I was also just too dog-tired to even think of doing anything just for myself.

But that's what writing is for me. It's my catharsis, my escape, my indulgence. Something that's mine and mine alone.

And God, does it feel good to have it back.

CHAPTER 1

Family, Friends, and Dutch Chefs

I have sometimes heard people say that their childhood was an unremarkable one, and I suppose the same could be said for mine – except that it *was* remarkable for me because it was mine.

Born in the summer of 1985, I was a happy accident, the second daughter of a couple who had suffered fertility issues before conceiving their first child – my older sister, Lizzie. I grew up on a quiet, sleepy street that still feels like home to me even now. The neighbours are still the same ones who watched us grow up and tear up and down the road on our bikes and, later, totter tipsily home on our stiletto heels (sounding "like a pack of horses clip-clopping down the street", as my dad used to say). It was a content and secure upbringing, and we were always a close family unit – we still are.

We were never going to be a wealthy family – Dad went out to work as a lorry driver while Mum was a stay-at-home parent – but we also never wanted for anything. Mum was always around and Dad only ever worked locally, which meant his commute was short and we saw a lot of him. He would start work early in the morning but was finished by four o'clock in the afternoon so he could be home just after we got back from school. At the weekends we had him all to ourselves.

The house was filled with laughter and books and toys. Granted, lots of the things we owned were second-hand or passed down from relatives, but in all honesty, no child cares about that. Lizzie and I were taught from an early age to use our imaginations and to make our own fun. We'd spend hours playing upstairs, inventing scenarios and acting them out. That way, Mum told us, we would never be bored.

Holidays were spent either in Wales or the New Forest in our little touring caravan. I don't think it really occurred to me to even want to go abroad when I was little. We had so much fun that a foreign holiday would have struggled to beat those golden days anyway. In my head, all those summers have now melted deliciously together to create one long, lazy holiday in the hazy sunshine, filled with laughter, ice cream, beaches, pen-pals, and first kisses.

Lizzie and I got on well for the most part, but like any siblings, we clashed from time to time. I cringe now when I remember how I used to tag along to wherever she was going with her friends – but if it annoyed her, she never let on. She was unbelievably patient with me. I idolised her and wanted to be just like her, although I would never have admitted it at the time. I'm still a little bit in awe of her now.

Every Saturday we would spend the day with Mum's parents, "Little" Granny and Grandad (we called them that for no reason we can fathom now). Little Granny was a Scotswoman with a tough exterior, but spending any length of time with her meant you'd soon see through the façade. Each week she would give me and Lizzie a bag of sweets each, and we would look forward to finding out what treats lay ahead for us that week. Often, there would be candy cigarettes (imagine that!) and we'd giggle as we pretended to smoke them, just to annoy Mum. Granny kept toys at the house for us and we were allowed free rein of the garden during the summer months. We were never bored there! In the afternoons, Mum and Granny would make tea for us all and I would sit with Grandad and help him mark off his football pools on the little slip he'd cut carefully out of the newspaper. Grandad was never overtly affectionate; it was in the little things like this that we knew he cared about us.

On Sundays it was Dad's parents' turn to host us. "Big" Granny and Grandad were heaps of fun and seemed eternally young. Their house had a huge back garden with an apple orchard that we'd spend hours in. I think a big part of my vast imagination was forged there. Big Granny loved to cook and bake for us all – I still miss her apple pies now. And Grandad was born into a family of boys whose forward-thinking mother had made sure they all knew how to take care of themselves. He could sew and was a fantastic cook – he loved making his famous "chippos" (potato fritters) for us all.

Jacob never knew either of my grandads, and he wasn't even two when we lost my grannies, but how they adored him! I talk to him about them all every day, and he says they are "angels in heaven now and Jesus is looking after them". Although sometimes he does get a bit mixed up and says, 'It's Granny Jesus!' when he sees a picture of one of them ...

*

I was one of those quite unique children who loved school. Primary school was all skipping-ropes, blue-and-white summer dresses, curiosity about the world, and the beginnings of my love for learning. But it was at secondary school that I really came into my own.

I was only in my first week there when I met Jen. I imagine it's quite rare in life to meet someone with exactly the same sense of humour as you (especially if that sense of humour is as niche as mine is), that person you only have to glance at to know immediately what they're thinking and can share a joke with without even uttering a word. Michael says it's like we've got our own language. But I did meet that person in Jen, and we became inseparable almost straightaway. From the first day we met, we would spend three hours on the phone to each other every night, much to my dad's annoyance. Little did he know that this was a pattern we would follow right up until we left college seven years later!

Mum and Dad used to pay for a deal with the landline, whereby you could phone another landline for up to an hour free of charge. If the call wasn't finished after the hour, you could simply hang up and re-dial the number and the next hour would be free too, and so on. Dad used to go mad because Jen and I never wanted to interrupt our conversation after the first hour, so I didn't hang up, meaning we had to pay for the rest of the time. When the itemised phone bill came through each month, the phone company used to highlight any numbers that had been called frequently or for particularly long calls by printing "chatter, chatter!" next to the number, which only served to draw Dad's attention to our marathon calls even more. Thanks for that, BT!

During that first year at my new school, Jen and I also became friends with Amanda, Nicole, Amy, Heather, and Becky. Amanda and Amy already knew each other from primary school. I warmed to Amy straightaway; she was so friendly and was always smiling, so it would have been difficult not to. Amanda was more reserved and I was convinced she didn't like me at first – she was very quiet and quite serious-looking for an 11-year-old (although she's the complete opposite as an adult!) – but once you reach the person inside, you realise that once she's your friend, she's your friend for life. Nicole was in my form class and we were bus buddies, listening to Westlife together each morning on the way to school. Heather is Amanda's younger sister and something of an acquired taste (I know she wouldn't mind me saying that). She always speaks her mind and is brutally honest. I'd hate to have her as an enemy, but am proud and blessed to be able to call her a friend. Becky now lives some distance away from the rest of us, but I still always know she's there if I need her. She's quite ditzy in everyday life, a lot like me, but is incredibly intelligent and hard-working when she needs to be.

Have you ever met a group of people who know you so completely that you can be totally, 100%, the absolute real version of yourself when you're with them? The version that hardly anyone else gets to see? I have, and I know I'm lucky.

My girls are as close to me as my family are. We have done all our growing up together and have this huge pool of shared memories that no one can ever take away. When I think of my friends, the overwhelming theme that springs to mind is laughter. Howling with laughter. Crying with laughter *all the time*. My friends are a lot of things, but "normal" they definitely are not! Neither am I, having said that. But who wants normal?

We used to have a girls' holiday every year (I like to think this will happen again once all the children – we have 10 between us – have upped and left). One of our first was, of course, the statutory jaunt to Blackpool when we were at Sixth Form. The "hotel" we stayed in was straight out of a low-budget horror film: dodgy paintings on every wall, sticky carpets on which we had to make paths out of newspaper before we could walk on them, and a hostess who cooked breakfast with one hand while smoking with the other.

Then there was the infamous budget cruise we took to Amsterdam. The boat was literally falling apart! Jen and I had to move rooms because our original one had a fly infestation. There was a hot tub on the deck, but it had long since stopped working properly, so we were given a hosepipe connected to boiling water so we could heat it ourselves.

We always seemed to meet a character or two on these jaunts, and this time it was Cookie, the elderly Dutch chef who always wore filthy chef's whites and seemed to be permanently drunk. One afternoon, as we were having a cocktail or two on board, he brought around some snacks and insisted that we try some, despite our protestations that we weren't hungry.

'Ooh, lovely,' we told him, trying to humour him. 'Is it mushroom? Cheese?'

'These are "bitterballs",' he said proudly. 'No mushroom, no cheese, just rented beef. Dutch snacks.'

We were literally speechless. *"Rented"? Maybe he meant "rendered"*? Either way, we had no clue!

Amy turned 22 while we were on the cruise. That night, in the bar, Cookie got wind of this and said he would make her a cake.

'No, no,' she protested, 'I'm fine.' But he had already gone.

He'd been gone for some time when I decided to go and have a look what he was doing. Peering round the kitchen door, I saw all the other kitchen staff darting about, trying to get dinner prepared. Cookie, who was oblivious to everything around him, was vigorously whisking Amy's cake in a bowl.

I crept back to the girls to reveal what I'd seen. 'He's actually making a cake from scratch!'

A few minutes later, Cookie burst out of the kitchen holding said "cake" at a very dangerous angle, swaying all over the deck as he shouted to the DJ to play 'Happy Birthday'. The DJ, clearly accustomed to Cookie's antics, obliged, but it started sooner than Cookie had expected and then changed to another song, so he shouted furiously, 'No! Play "'appy birthday"!' in very broken English.

When the song came back on, Cookie made a beeline for Amy with his confectionery creation, which was now worryingly complete with lit candles and sparklers. It seemed to be partly frozen. He made us all try a piece and we had to pretend we were really enjoying it, but when his back was turned, we tried to get rid of as much of it as we could in various plant pots and vases. Jen and Amy were still up at six in the morning, and they swear blind that Cookie left the party just before six and then came back ten minutes later. He'd got changed into some different, but equally dirty, chef's whites and began to prepare for the breakfast shift!

During our student years, we used to go "out out" to the local town twice a week without fail. It wasn't exactly what you would call a "classy" night out, and we could often be found trawling the bars in a whole spectrum of different fancy-dress outfits. In our time we have been nurses, builders (complete with tool belts), Mrs Clauses, firefighters (on that particular occasion we came complete with a hired fire engine that acted as our taxi for the evening) ... you name it, we've worn it!

We became inexplicably obsessed with the little road-sweepers that would come and start to clean the roads even before the last revellers had gone home (why does everything seem so much funnier when you're drunk?). Scarab Minors, they were called. Or at least, that's what was painted on the side of them. We vowed that we would one day ride through the streets in a Scarab, so we started to become friendly with the men who drove them. Then, one glorious night, they invited us inside. There were seven of us squeezed into the little cab, along with the two men, and we really felt like we'd made it.

'I bet you ladies wouldn't go on a date with us?' the men joked. *What, all seven of us?*

'You're joking!' Jen piped up. 'One glass of Lambrini and we're anyone's!'

All these shared experiences have cemented our friendship over the years. Now, I couldn't be without any one of them.

CHAPTER 2

No Spinning Please!

I think it would be fair to say that I have always had something of an obsessive personality. From a young age, I would compulsively wash my hands in spite of the fact that it made my eczema worse; my hands would often be dry, cracked, and bleeding and still I wasn't deterred. Mum tried to discourage me from this excessive washing simply by saying that I didn't need to do it, but it didn't stop me.

'You don't need to do that,' she would say. 'Just tell yourself to stop doing it.'

'But it's not that easy,' I would argue back.

'It is.'

And then the conversation would be finished, because neither of us was willing to accept the other's viewpoint.

I don't feel angry towards Mum at all for this; her nature is such that she always just wants to make everything okay for everyone, so she wants to try to solve all our problems as quickly as she can.

I thought I could prevent bad things from happening to my family by continuing with my rituals. If not, at least I'd have tried my best and only wasted a few extra minutes a day, whereas if I failed to carry them out and something bad *did* happen, I'd only have myself to blame.

I don't think that anyone else really noticed my rituals, or at least they never mentioned it. They would probably have just dismissed them as a phase if they had. There was no history of mental ill-health in my family so there would have been nothing to compare it to, I suppose.

The hand-washing lessened over time and was replaced with new obsessions – turning my light switch off and on sixteen times before I went to sleep, touching the dining table a certain number of times before leaving it, or trying the handle of the back door eight or sixteen times to make sure it was properly locked before going out. Everything was done either four times or in multiples of four, which I didn't think much about in those days. Sixteen was my favoured number because it was four times four; a nice square number. I felt that these compulsions didn't really affect my life too much at that time, so I wasn't inclined to seek help or talk to anyone about them particularly.

Other manifestations of my (as yet) undiagnosed OCD included quite complex word games in my head, which I still play now, particularly in times of stress. If I hear or read a sentence, I have to break it down and rearrange it so that it fits in better with my number four obsession. For example, the sentence 'Humpty Dumpty sat on a wall' would have to be rearranged in my head to:

'On wall Humpty Dumpty sat a.'

This means that all the even-numbered words (which I favour) are at the beginning of the sentence (smallest words first, bigger ones last) and the horrible odds are at the end (strangely enough, I never considered this when giving my son a five-lettered first name!). Then I would need to sort them further to make words of four letters:

'Onwa llHu mpty Dump tysa ta.'

Finally, because there's still a pesky two-letter word at the end of the sentence, I would need to add another two-letter word in there to round it off to four. So I might say:

'Oh, Humpty Dumpty sat on a wall.'

Then change it to:

'Oh on wall Humpty Dumpty sat a.'

Then:

'Ohon wall Hump tyDu mpty sata.'

But then that still wouldn't be quite right because there are only seven words in the sentence, and the number of words in the sentence needs to be even as well. Strangely, it doesn't need to be four words or a multiple of four, just as long as it's an even number. So, six would be fine, but in this instance I'd round it up to eight. So I might say:

'Oh, Humpty Dumpty sat on a wall, yeah.'

'Ohon wall yeah Hump tyDu mpty sata.'

And that would be my finished sentence.

It wouldn't matter that the finished sentence is only seven words long because it's made up of eight words originally. And if that messes with your head, imagine what it does to mine having to go through this daily! Of course, I don't do it with every sentence I hear or see, but usually do if it's an isolated phrase rather than being part of a longer conversation or text.

If I need to turn around, say, to talk to someone, I always have to turn back the same way I came so that I haven't done a "spin", so to speak. I'm howling with laughter writing this because it sounds so ridiculous when I put it down on paper, but makes perfect sense to me at the time when it's happening! So please don't feel bad if you're laughing too; I'm still just a normal person who likes to take the mickey out of myself sometimes.

And it goes on. I try to find symmetrical patterns in wallpaper. Sometimes I have a compulsion to look at objects or people a certain number of times (usually four), which probably makes people think I'm staring at them when really I'm not.

When I was around 16, I became obsessed with the idea that I might be sick in public if I ate too much. I restricted what I ate when out and about to such an extent that I would perhaps only order a small portion of fries when I went to McDonald's with friends, or eat only a few mouthfuls from my plate in a restaurant. If I felt I had eaten too much, I would become very hot and anxious and feel as though I was going to be sick. I was always trying to locate the nearest toilet as quickly as possible whenever I went anywhere new. Strangely, my large teenage appetite would magically restore itself once I was back at home and in my own familiar surroundings, and I could handle other people being sick. It was the loss of control over my body that I hated, the idea of having that terrible churning feeling and knowing for sure that I was about to be sick that terrified me.

But sometimes, if I was feeling particularly anxious about something, I would make myself sick on purpose after eating as a way to try to purge my body of my worries. It wasn't every day and I certainly don't claim to have had an eating disorder in the way that some people suffer from them, but I definitely think it was part of my OCD and my constant battle for perfectionism. I didn't want to feel any anxiety as this would mean I was imperfect, so I would do whatever I could to try to get rid of these feelings. This went on for a couple of years, until I became settled and secure in my relationship with Michael, when my weight went from around six stone to a much healthier eight stone for my 5'8" frame.

I still have a somewhat strange relationship with food from time to time. During periods of stress, I tend to either not eat at all or completely stuff my face, and then feel incredibly guilty about it afterwards. I obsess over the fat on my tummy and under my chin, and I constantly look at my reflection to see how noticeable it is.

I can't say that I wish I didn't have OCD, because I don't know what it's like not to have it; it's just a part of me. It's who I am.

But perhaps it would be nice to find out. Just for a day.

Because having OCD is bloody exhausting sometimes.

CHAPTER 3

A Manly Man and a Curly Cat

It was in 2005, while I was studying for my degree, that I met the man with whom I would spend the rest of my life.

The first time I set eyes on my future husband, I was in a club I used to go to a lot with my friends, and he was dancing with the kind of joyous abandon one usually only sees in small children. I liked that about him – he didn't seem to notice or care what other people thought of him.

I was attracted to him straightaway; he was tall, good-looking, and self-assured, with the broad-shouldered, rugby-player-type physique that I like. He had beautiful hazel eyes and the longest eyelashes ever. I didn't think I stood a chance! Michael seemed really confident with girls, so whenever he flirted with me, I just thought it was what he did with everyone and tried not to take it too seriously (even though I secretly hoped he saw me differently).

I think it's fair to say that I did quite a bit of the chasing (one night quite literally round a bar trying to kiss him, as Jen likes to remind me). He did eventually ask me out, however, and we went to a local wine bar; he came to meet me one Sunday afternoon after my shift at Claire's Accessories finished. I never quite forgave my colleagues for crowding round the window to get a good look at him as we started to walk off!

I'd been worried we'd be stuck for conversation as we had only ever seen each other after a few drinks up until then, but I was surprised at how easy it was – it was as though we'd already been dating for a while.

We became a couple very quickly after that first date. We didn't realise at the time, but Michael and I had actually been at secondary school together (although he's three years older), and he was friends with a group of people with whom we had become friendly through college. I joke now that we'd never have got together if I'd known him in those days; he was something of a rascal at school from what he tells me. I, on the other hand, was a bit of a nerd, and proud of it. (I was the type of student who would offer to go in and help the teachers at lunchtime just for fun!)

My friends were wary at first as Michael had a reputation for fighting, but they were soon reassured when they saw how happy I was, and how our relationship started to soften his nature. Michael cuts quite an imposing figure with his height and broad stature, but is actually really soft and cries more when watching *E.T.* than I do!

Ever since we first became a couple, Michael has treated me like a princess, and I never doubt how lucky I am to have him. He's generally happy as long as I am, and is very easy-going, which means I usually get to pick where we go for dinner or what film we're going to watch. On a practical level, such as when it comes to money and savings, he is definitely the more sensible out of the two of us and will always rein me in if I start spending too much. My trouble is that I want to be involved in everything and anything – *girls' weekend away? Count me in! Impromptu cocktail evening? Yes, please!* – so we kind of balance each other out, I suppose.

Three years after we got together, we bought our first house and quickly made it a home. We soon completed the nest with our very own Devon Rex kitten called Teddy, a beautiful wavy-haired feline with a heavenly, soft, chocolate smoke-coloured coat. He was an absolute ball of energy and mischief (some people refer to Rexes as "monkeys in cat suits") and we loved him fiercely from the off.

Life in our first home was blissful for the first few years. I worked as a library assistant in a local library, and then later as a school librarian, the job I still hold. It was after a discussion with some university friends that I decided this was the field I wanted to work in. It seemed to fit in perfectly with both my love of literature and my methodical mindset. Michael was a security guard at a factory not far from our home. We lived close to my parents and close to Michael's dad, saw our friends regularly, and had some wonderful holidays. Before he met me, Michael had never been out of the country – barely out of the city, even – but I am a certified sun-lover and have brought him round by taking him on plenty of beach holidays. Our favourite place to go to is Turkey.

Michael proposed on my 24th birthday. It wasn't entirely unexpected; I'd been dropping hints for months beforehand.

'I like rings,' I would say, holding up my ring finger to show him, 'but I haven't got one for this finger. It feels a bit empty.'

Michael had planned a special evening for the proposal. He was going to take me out for a meal at our favourite Italian restaurant next to the canal and intended to stoop down on one knee as we walked amongst the twinkly lights next to the water afterwards.

Unfortunately for him, I changed my mind at the last minute about the restaurant because the original one told us they had a large party in that night and I preferred something a bit quieter, so we ended up in an equally lovely but very different place in the middle of town instead. With no twinkly lights in sight, the proposal took place in the hallway of our little house once we got back home.

'Will you marry me?' Michael asked nervously as he got down on one knee.

'Yes!' I shrieked. 'But I need to go for a wee first!'

It wasn't quite what either of us had in mind, but we were both overjoyed to be engaged at last.

We immediately set a date for 19th May 2012, giving us three years to plan the wedding. We made arrangements at a leisurely pace, quaffing champagne at every opportunity, browsing wedding fayres and subscribing to all the bridal magazines – it became our new hobby. By the time the big day arrived, we had been together for seven years and were as ready as we could be for the next chapter of our lives to commence.

CHAPTER 4

Dreams Begin to Crumble Like Wedding Cake

The years ambled idly by, almost without us realising. Our relationship had been easy and uncomplicated until that point; there had been nothing to worry over or to test the strength of our bond.

Our wedding day finally dawned one crisp and clear May morning, seven years after that first date. We had a beautiful service conducted in our local Catholic church, attended by everyone we love and followed by a reception in a large country house not far from our home. My dress was a Grecian-style gown – one-shouldered and straight, with some simple detailing at the waist. I'm tall but quite delicately framed, so I hadn't wanted a dress that would drown me, and this seemed the perfect option. My flowers were simple too: white lilies that I carried draped over my arm rather than in a traditional bouquet.

On the morning of the wedding, everyone seemed to be rushing around in a frenzy, but I was very calm. Dad and I were sitting eating a full English breakfast when Jen (who was to be my maid of honour) bowled into my parents' house early that morning. She has always treated the place like a second home.

'Neil!' she yelled at Dad, impatiently tapping the meticulous schedule she'd typed out for us, with timings planned out to the minute. 'The schedule says you're supposed to be in the shower now! What the hell are you doing?!'

Dad and I just looked at each other and laughed as we ignored her and carried on eating.

And that was the pattern the rest of the day was to follow: relaxed, casual, and easy-going. I think that part of my composure was because I knew I was marrying the right man; there had never been any doubt in my mind that this was what I wanted.

*

Following the wedding, we took a honeymoon to Ibiza, which I now look back on with a certain wistfulness. We were so carefree back then, with no worries about what was to come.

I distinctly remember talking about having children during the honeymoon. We were sitting in a quiet little bar by the seafront, the days of our lives stretching out blissfully in front of us. There was a young girl singing at the front of the bar. They were songs that we knew, but she had a kind of haunting, ethereal quality to her voice, and so an air of calm and tranquillity had settled over the place.

When Michael and I first met, he had always been adamant that he never wanted children. He admits he was quite immature until he met me, so he had never imagined that settling down and starting a family would be on the agenda. As far as he could see, he would always be the party boy he was back then. He says this changed soon after he met me; he had finally found someone he was serious about and wanted a future with, and soon came around to thinking about a life with children in it.

As for me, I have always been very maternal. I was the one that my friends had pegged as having children first, even back when we were at school. From a very early age, I have been drawn towards babies and smaller children and I have quite a motherly, protective nature. I'm almost sure this comes from my own mum, who is very similar in this way. I was always open about the fact that I saw myself as a stay-at-home mum rather than a career woman, and I made this clear to Michael almost as soon as I realised we were going to be serious.

I wanted to come off my contraceptive pill straightaway, but Michael wanted to wait for a few months until we'd saved up a bit more money. My lovely, solid husband was trying to be sensible as usual. But I had a nagging feeling somewhere deep down that we might struggle to conceive, as had been the case with my mum and dad some 31 years earlier, when they received treatment to help conceive my older sister, Lizzie.

At this point, I hadn't really explored the details of this treatment with them – it had simply never come up in our conversations. All I knew was that they had needed assistance with Lizzie, so I'd always had the thought at the back of my mind that I might have problems too. I'd also voiced this to Michael fairly early on in the relationship. We both agreed that we wanted to be married before starting a family, so we had to put those concerns to the back of our minds until that day came.

This became harder as the years went by and friends of ours started to have babies. I think that was probably partly why we were still fairly young when we got married; at 26 and 29, we knew we might not be able to afford to hang around.

In the end, we decided I should come off the pill as soon as we returned home. I think Michael had always just assumed it would happen straightaway at a time of our choosing, but after speaking to him about what my parents went through and several other couples I knew, he quickly realised that few people actually have the luxury of getting pregnant as soon as they feel like it. We knew that we needed to get a move on if we were to be the young parents we dreamt of being, able to keep up with our children and to have the energy to invest in them.

Those first few months of trying were exciting and full of hope – it was like a little secret we had just between the two of us, and I loved the feeling that I could be pregnant at any time but just didn't know it yet. I would often imagine that my tummy looked rounder or that I was feeling pregnancy symptoms and would spend hours painstakingly looking up the signs of pregnancy on the parenting websites, trying to convince myself that a twitch in my eye or getting dry lips meant that I was absolutely, definitely pregnant. But I never was. It was never my time.

Why wasn't my body doing what it was built to do? Friends of ours seemed to be announcing their pregnancies almost daily, and yet our turn didn't come. I remember how it felt trying to look over the moon when people told me their fabulous news. And I was genuinely happy for them, don't get me wrong. It just felt like I'd been punched in the stomach each time. I would go home and sob through the night for the baby we longed for.

Michael was understandably upset too, but tried to stay strong for me. He would hold me while I cried and tell me everything would be okay. I think he felt that if he broke down too, we might just both fall apart and then where would we be? I realise now that he bottled a lot of his feelings up, but I was too wrapped up in my own grief to see it. I wish I could go back now and be the one holding him for a change. It makes me wonder if he ever really dealt with those feelings or whether I never gave him the chance to.

Almost a year after we had started trying for a family, Michael and I felt we just needed to get away and have a break from all things babies. We rented a cottage in the Peak District and decided to forget everything for a while. On the morning we arrived there, I answered a phone call from my dad. He wanted to tell me about a family member who had just announced their pregnancy after experiencing previous miscarriages. I tried to sound as happy for them as I could, but the tears were already coming before I put the phone down. The timing was so bad, it was almost comical.

That afternoon, Michael and I went to a small village pub and I drank more wine than I should have done. On the way back to the cottage, I tripped and fell flat on my face, cutting myself in several places. As Michael helped me to my feet, I started to cry uncontrollably – not because of the fall, but because my heart just ached so much.

The expectations of those around us were also difficult to deal with. Newlyweds are routinely asked by all and sundry when they will be starting a family, and it's just assumed that it will happen easily. I completely understand why – it's because family and friends love you and are excited to be a part of your new life together, and that usually includes children. It's also because most people love babies. I've even asked these questions of people myself in the past. But it doesn't hurt any less when you're desperate for a baby but are struggling to conceive and are being asked daily if there is any news. It felt like we were letting everyone down by never having anything to announce. I would constantly brush away the comments, saying that we didn't want children yet and that we wanted to enjoy just being married for a while first.

Looking back, I should have just been honest, but I was frightened of making people feel awkward or uncomfortable, so I let myself suffer instead. Now, with the benefit of hindsight, I make a point of never asking young couples these questions and I would love others to consider doing the same – you just never know how much you could be hurting someone without even realising.

Once, we were at a family party with Lizzie and her children. We were being introduced to some friends of my auntie's and Lizzie was going through the names and ages of her brood as she introduced them all. Then, one of the ladies we were talking to turned to me and asked, 'Don't you want children?'

I had no answer prepared and felt myself getting hot as I squirmed under all the watching eyes. I managed to stutter something about there being plenty of time yet, but my evening was ruined and I took myself off to the bathroom for a good cry as soon as I could get away.

Another time, I was at a friend's baby shower when another guest asked, 'Will it be your turn next then?'

Again, I gave my stock answer of there being bags of time for that and legged it as soon as I could. The only way I could get through the rest of the baby shower at least slightly intact was to neck a bottle of wine on my own in the kitchen.

But possibly the worst thing that was ever said to me, and I beg others to please never say this to anyone else, was during a conversation about a friend's parents and in-laws both wanting to see the grandchildren on Christmas day and the arguments that had happened due to this. I said that I'd be inclined to do whatever suited the children best at the time and was told, in no uncertain terms, 'You won't understand until you've got children.'

I felt an inch tall. Every other person in that conversation was already a parent. Most hadn't started trying for a baby until after me, yet here I was being told that my opinion wasn't valid because I wasn't a parent. I was so hurt, and I still feel that hurt to this day whenever I think about it. It's still quite painful to recall.

Just over a year after we started trying, I decided to go and see my GP. I know that some couples try for a lot longer before seeking help, but my impatience had got the better of me, and I also knew a little about why we hadn't conceived by this point. After another tough evening of sitting through a pregnancy announcement and trying to hide my heartbreak behind my smiles, I finally confided in a friend of mine about our fertility struggles. To my amazement, this friend was going through almost exactly the same thing and had also been present at the announcement that evening.

'I'm really happy for them. I'm just finding it hard because we've been trying to have a baby for a year now and have had no luck.'

'I'm in a similar position,' she replied. 'It's been 10 months for us. It's like I'm so happy for them, but so sad for me, and that feels selfish.'

'I know exactly what you mean,' I reassured her.

We hugged for the longest time and the relief of actually sharing my burden with someone else was immediate and intense. I was no longer alone and now had someone to cry to other than Michael, who was so busy supporting me that he wasn't looking after his own emotions about our infertility.

My friend recommended the book *Taking Charge of Your Fertility* by Toni Weschler, which I duly bought. From the book, I taught myself all about how to understand my own fertility: the cycle it goes through each month and the ways to determine if there may be problems. I wanted to make sure I had good grounds for going to the doctor before booking my appointment, so that he'd have no choice but to listen to me. I felt like I was at last starting to take charge of the body that had been letting me down.

I marched determinedly into the surgery, armed with all the basal body temperature charts I'd been keeping to track my ovulation. From the reading I'd been doing around conception, I'd discovered from tracking my temperature each day (a thermometer up the backside proved to be the most reliable method – I was willing to try anything!) that I was not ovulating. The body temperature is supposed to peak just after ovulation has occurred, whereas mine was staying at a pretty constant temperature throughout the month.

My lack of ovulation was confirmed by a series of blood tests, which took place over several consecutive months. I felt time was ticking away – why were we messing around with blood tests when I already knew what the results would tell us? Once the confirmation came, it was a relief, more than anything else, that I now knew there was a legitimate reason that I wasn't pregnant. Michael, on the other hand, was angry and heartbroken and felt it was so unfair. For some reason, he felt he'd let me down, even though it was my body that was failing. He says he was taken by surprise as he realised how much he actually wanted this, when just a few years earlier it had never crossed his mind that he'd want to be a dad. He didn't want to be the token infertile couple amongst our friends. I'm quite a logical person as a rule so I just wanted to know how we could fix it, how long it would take, and when we would have our positive pregnancy test.

But, of course, it doesn't always work that way and it would take months of me taking Clomid (a drug specifically designed to help stimulate ovulation) before I was finally found to be ovulating. I've always had faith in science and medicine, so I was willing to try anything that was suggested to us. I jumped at the chance to take the Clomid; I was so desperate to just get on with starting a family, and saw it as a means to an end rather than a biological failing.

During this time, I was still charting my temperatures, and I discovered myself that the luteal phase of my cycle was far too short to result in a pregnancy. The luteal phase is the part of the menstrual cycle that happens after ovulation, when the egg has already been released from the ovaries, but before the period begins. During the luteal phase, the uterus lining should have enough time to thicken in preparation for a pregnancy, but if this phase is too short, the lining doesn't have the chance to thicken enough and so the embryo cannot attach itself to the uterus wall. Once ovulation has occurred, the body temperature should be around a degree higher than during pre-ovulation, in order for a pregnancy to occur. In short, even though I was now releasing an egg, it was unlikely any fertilised egg would have enough time to attach to the wall of the uterus before my period began.

At about the same time that I found out about the luteal phase, Michael was also receiving the results back of some semen analysis that he'd had done privately. Unfortunately, these showed that his sperm motility was very low and that the quality of his sperm was poor. His sperm count was also quite low. Michael managed to stay quite positive despite this news. He held on to the fact that he was still relatively young and that things could improve with time, whereas for me it was yet another big blow. He was advised to change his lifestyle, namely a healthier diet and more exercise, and to have the test repeated in a few months' time, which he did.

The second sperm analysis came back even worse than the first and we had no clear idea as to why, which was frustrating to say the least, although it may have been due to a testicular varicocele that he later had removed. Although not proven, there are certain schools of thought that suggest this procedure can have a positive impact on fertility. When the varicocele was discovered, it seemed to me as though things just kept getting worse and we were getting further and further away from our dream of having a baby. It was yet another hurdle and something else we would need to wait months to see resolved. It was like those dreams you have where you're rushing to get somewhere and more and more things keep holding you up. Michael was also frustrated.

'Not something else,' he groaned when we found out.

Shockingly, this attitude comes from professionals too. One dismissive consultant told us to forget about children for now and try again in a few years.

'You're still young,' he said. 'Things might be different in a few years' time.'

I felt like shaking him – it was possibly the worst thing he could have said to two people so desperate for a baby. I'll never forget the look of devastation on Michael's face.

My husband still gets angry now whenever we talk about it; he says he could have happily put his fist through a wall that day. I have never seen him so angry. He felt – and feels – that there was absolutely no compassion or understanding for our situation;

the doctor said it so flippantly and he was so dismissive of us. Doctors are supposed to be there to talk to – how could we ever trust one again after this? And how could we forget about the one thing we yearned for above everything else?

By this time, we were beginning to feel quite desperate. We had always talked about the possibility of adoption, even if we had been able to have biological children, so this was the next natural step for us. We both felt that we could love a child that wasn't biologically our own just as much as if we were birth parents.

We also felt that the assisted conception (IVF/IUI) route was not for us. Michael completely understood why I did not want to put either of us through this. With less than a one in three chance of success and often painful physical and psychological side effects – as I'd seen firsthand in some of our family members and friends – I wasn't sure we were strong enough for it. I admire those who are.

So, very slowly, very cautiously, we turned towards the only light we could see. Adoption.

CHAPTER 5

Proceeding with Caution

From the time we received our initial adoption information pack in the post, right through to when we were approved to adopt 10-month-old identical twins, we never once wavered in the belief that this was the right path for us. Although the adoption process can be intrusive, scary, and exhausting, we carried on with the end goal in our sight: the family we so desperately wanted.

Having said this, there was a certain grieving process that we had to go through first. I found it difficult to accept that I would never experience pregnancy, birth, or breastfeeding. Even later on in the adoption process, I would feel a physical ache when I saw a pregnant woman in the street. It was almost as though my mouth would water with the longing for a biological child. I think that's something that probably always stays with a woman (and, to a degree, a man) who is not able to have a baby in the traditional way. I seemed to see pregnant women and babies everywhere – it was like having a constant reminder of what my body should have been able to do but couldn't. There was a stage when I became ashamed of my body, of my flat stomach and narrow hips, because I thought they gave away the fact that I had never carried a child. I even began to worry that people would guess we were adopters straightaway, just by looking at me. But

I knew I had to try to get over these feelings if we were to ever complete our family.

The first step, which took place in the summer of 2013, was to attend a meeting for prospective adopters, run by our local authority. Michael and I were nervous but excited as we entered the room. There were about 20 people there in total, from all different walks of life. Some were older couples, others were around the same age as us, and yet others were very young, perhaps only in their early twenties. There was also a handful of single people there, both men and women. I appreciated the diverse mix of characters; there was something comforting in realising that, while you need to be a woman of a certain age to conceive a child naturally, in theory almost any demographic can adopt.

I felt I had found my people. We didn't get the opportunity to talk amongst ourselves, so we couldn't swap details and stay in touch at this stage, but I still felt a sense of solidarity in the room. I wasn't being judged for what my womb could or couldn't produce and, in return, I wasn't there to judge them.

The evening ran to a strict and full schedule, and we learnt a lot at that first meeting, particularly about the children in our area who needed adoptive parents. It turns out that our city has an unusually high rate of babies with adoption orders compared to much of the rest of the country. I think we both had mixed feelings about that; it was sad to think of all those tiny children waiting for parents, but it also made us feel hopeful that we would find a child who was the right match for us.

We learnt that boys are harder to place than girls, but this didn't matter – we had always pictured ourselves with boys. I'm hopeless with hairstyles, for one thing, and I love the rough-and-tumble way that lots of boys play. I've also seen gorgeously close relationships between mums and their boys, and liked the idea of having the same for myself.

We also found out that sibling groups are harder to place. The thought of adopting siblings had never even occurred to us; we felt that we would have enough to contend with in adopting one, since we had no experience in parenting!

We were told that anyone who had undergone fertility treatment would need to demonstrate that they had fully come to terms with not having a biological child before they could embark on the adoption process. This excluded us, however, as we had decided to bypass IVF (the Clomid wasn't counted). Pets also needed to be considered - would they be a suitable housemate for a child?

Even though there was clearly a lot for us to think about, that first meeting really just reinforced to us the fact that this was the right path for us; nothing that was said had made us feel put-off or wary - we were only more determined to begin the process.

Next, we had a home visit from two social workers who carried out an initial assessment on our house to make sure it was suitable for a child to move into - checking that it had sufficient bedrooms, that it was safe and clean etc. Although we'd been told not to clean the house especially for the visit (the social workers wanted to see it as it usually was), we of course spent the whole morning scrubbing it from top to bottom. We were definitely nervous about the visit, but also excited and keen to make a start. We felt ready.

The visit also involved us answering some basic questions about ourselves: our upbringings, our reasons for choosing adoption etc. We then had to wait for a couple of weeks to see whether we could formally move onto stage one of the process - a wait which seemed to go on forever.

Once we were given the green light to move to the next stage, we decided that it was time to tell all our family and friends. In a way, it felt like this was the beginning of a pregnancy for me - an unconventional one, yes, but it was my version of being pregnant. True, things could still go wrong, but the same could be said for the prenatal period anyway.

What we should have remembered was that we'd had months to get used to the idea, while the people we told were only now hearing about it for the first time. Absolutely everyone we told was over the moon for us. Some were shocked about our infertility and commiserated with us. But, once it had sunk in, everyone really rallied round and supported us to the full.

I was equally overwhelmed by the support I received at work. My co-workers were so excited for me! I have colleagues who have been through the same process and who were happy to talk about it and offer advice. Most people had lots of questions, which I would have gladly spent all day answering – after all, this was my version of a pregnancy, so I was pleased that people were interested and wanted to talk about it!

Stage one of the adoption process involves exploring adoption in detail and working out what difficulties our prospective children might be facing. Even if you end up adopting a baby rather than an older child, there are still a wealth of possibilities for problems as some things are set in stone while still in the womb – foetal alcohol syndrome, mental health problems, learning difficulties, attachment issues ... the list goes on and on. At the end of each meeting during this first stage, Michael and I would go over what had been spoken about and decide together what we thought we could and couldn't cope with, such as terminal illness or chronic physical and mental health conditions. We both really appreciated the honesty demonstrated by the social workers when talking about these potential issues – I always feel like it's best to be given the worst-case scenario from the off so that you can be at least a little prepared.

We were encouraged to carry out our own extensive reading and research on adopted children and their potential issues. I got right back into my researcher mindset and made notes and notes and more notes detailing each possible scenario. We learnt how brain development can differ in children whose parental attachments have been broken or interfered with. Some people (admittedly, us included) who have no experience of adoption tend to be of the belief that by adopting a baby you can "mould" their personality, and that they won't remember their early days or life inside the womb. The reality is actually very different – the damage unfortunately will have already been done. As well as the effects of potential drug and alcohol abuse, others factors are at play too. Research has shown that abandonment and rejection can be felt by babies in utero, and that this early loss of the biological parent often leads to anxiety disorders and depression later in life. We start our path of learning and feeling while still in the womb; chaotic surroundings, stress, and abuse can be felt by the foetus and this can lead to a marked increase in the stress hormone cortisol and can impact on the baby's sense of self-worth. Early brain development can also be affected by these traumas.

We were told about the situations in which many of the children would have been with their birth parents, such as sexual, emotional, and physical abuse, neglect, or living in environments where drug and alcohol addiction was commonplace. We learnt that these situations aren't always black-and-white; often, the birth parents will have been raised in similar circumstances and simply don't know how to parent effectively – it's not always just that they don't love their children. Cycles can be impossible to break sometimes. For example, one story we were told was of a little boy, aged three, who had habitually been sexually abused by a family friend. His mother had knowingly let this happen because the same thing had happened to her when she was a child so she didn't see anything out of the ordinary with it.

These stories were heartbreaking, of course, but they just made us all the more determined to see the process through. Our child was out there, and we were damned if we weren't going to find them!

The meetings also told us about contact with the child's birth family, which can differ on a case-by-case basis. The most common form of contact is through the local authority's postbox service, whereby birth parents, birth siblings, adoptive parents, and children can keep in contact through letters, usually once a year.

The overwhelming aim with modern adoption is to ensure that the child always knows that they are adopted, rather than finding out later in life, which could have a major impact on mental health and can lead to a crisis of identity. The notion of adoption will be introduced to them as soon as they are able to understand it, and the rest of their story is drip-fed to them as they become more curious and want to know more. These days, there are all sorts of books you can buy around the topic of adoption so that adopted children don't see themselves as being alone or "different". The child's story, however, is exactly that: it's *theirs*, and they will always have access to their life story as and when they want it. It's absolutely key to their sense of identity.

Michael and I both felt really positive about this; we acknowledged that it's best all round to be open and honest. If the child has always known about their origins, there are no big surprises. Difficult conversations, yes, but no major shocks. Our child would always know that they had a "birth mum" and a "birth dad" as well as us (their mum and dad), and would be told all about their birth family as they grew up.

We felt prepared and empowered by the research and by talking to other adopters, absorbing every documentary and book we could devour on the subject. The adoption journey (quite rightly) takes over your whole world.

The second stage of the process is a detailed study on the prospective adoptive parents: us. I have friends who have adopted children (I got to know them during our adoption process – lots of the training is done in groups so that you build up a support network of people in the same situation as you) and I know that some people can find this part of the process extremely difficult and draining. It intrudes on your innermost emotions and digs away at your past until the social workers have a complete picture of you as a person and how you came to be as you are. I think it was mainly due to the sensitivity and compassion of our two allocated social workers, Andrea and Karen, that I actually quite enjoyed this part – putting our family trees together, re-visiting my happy childhood, and opening up about my dreams for my future children. I can imagine that it would be much harder on a person whose childhood had not been so good, however.

Almost from the start of the adoption process, both Michael and I agreed that we would prefer to adopt a baby rather than an older child. As a relatively young couple, we both wanted the "baby experience" and felt that we could offer a really good support network to a younger child, partly due to the fact that lots of our friends had very young babies and children at the time. They would be able to give lots of practical advice and provide our child with an immediate circle of friends. It's not really possible to adopt a very young baby, as the process of granting an adoption order from a judge takes time, so six months of age is usually the youngest that a child can be adopted.

As part of the process, you are asked to complete a questionnaire about the types of issues you would be willing to take on. I remember bursting into tears when I ticked "no" against the question that asked if we would consider a child with a life-limiting illness.

'But who would tick "yes" to that?' I asked Andrea.

'There are people. Usually people who have experience of dealing with those kinds of illnesses already.'

Nevertheless, I still felt terrible guilt for saying I wouldn't consider this. What if the child that was supposed to be ours had such an illness, and here I was discounting them out-of-hand because I didn't think I could cope with that? I think we both believed that there was one child out there that was supposed to be ours, so how awful would it be if we were to say, 'Thanks, but no thanks' to our destined child!

As the process went on, we both agreed we would try to remain open-minded as to what we would be willing to do. Having said this, we were adamant that we didn't want to see the profiles of any children before being officially approved as adopters, just in case something went wrong. I have seen the fallout that ensues when this happens, and it's truly devastating.

Our adoption approval panel took place during the summer of 2014. There were about 10 people assessing our suitability as adoptive parents, including social workers, adopters, people who had been adopted, and medical professionals. It took a whole morning of waiting to see the panel before we finally went in. I don't remember being nervous – I was confident of the research we had done and of our reasons for wanting to adopt, so it just felt like more of a friendly chat, and the panel were all lovely and encouraging. We spoke about the different physical and mental health issues we might be dealing with, how we would deal with children who had been through specific kinds of abuse, and how well we would be supported. They wanted to know about the relationships I had with other adopters, ones we had met through the adoption process and others who were friends and colleagues. In the end, we were unanimously approved and couldn't wait to get outside to phone everyone and tell them our news.

Things progressed relatively quickly after that. Andrea showed us the profile for twin boys, aged eight months, who she thought would be a good match for us. On the photograph they were sitting side-by-side, supported with cushions as they were unable to sit unaided at that point. They weren't smiling and actually looked a bit bemused, as though they knew they were waiting for their new parents but didn't know who they were going to be and when they would get to meet them. How could we not start to fall in love once we'd seen the photograph and read about their favourite toys and songs?

We had already stated to our social workers that we might be willing to adopt twins if we felt we were the right fit for them (and that's important too – adoption is about providing families for children, not children that will fit neatly into families).

We met with the doctor who had been on our approval panel and she talked us through some of their physical and developmental issues and their potential learning difficulties. There was nothing she said that we felt we couldn't take on.

We read extensively into the twins' background, which I can't go into, but parts of it made us both weep. It felt like we were getting more and more attached to them the more we learnt.

Just before Christmas 2014, we attended a "matching panel" (similar to the approval panel, except this time it's to approve you to adopt specific children). We were asked questions about our support network and how comfortable we would feel phoning people for help in the middle of the night. How would we make sure the boys learnt about their heritage and birth family? How did we feel about taking on their additional physical and developmental needs? How would we feel about future mental health issues or learning difficulties arising? We answered each question with thought and care – we had discussed all these issues with our social workers in the weeks leading up to this, so we felt well prepared. Again, we were unanimously approved to adopt the twins, and this set the ball well and truly rolling. To make it even more special, a friend from work who had been going through the same process was approved to adopt her child on the same day! We had been through each stage at almost exactly the same time, so we could offer plenty of support to each other. It meant so much to be able to share our journeys!

The twins' social worker came to our house to see what the set-up was. We were sent lots of photos of them over the Christmas period and started to set the house up ready for their arrival. It was finally starting to feel real. We were going to be parents at last! It felt like we were becoming part of a club, a secret society that we'd never been allowed into before: The Parents Club. Now, we could finally join in with all the conversations we'd previously felt excluded from, and would have our own babies to show off to the world, rather than fussing over everyone else's. We were almost Mum and Dad at last, and it felt so right.

We were the happiest we'd been in a long time. We'd not dared buy anything for the babies before the approval panel in case something went wrong, but now we felt free to shop for beautiful clothes, cots, car seats, a travel system, and all the other paraphernalia that comes with being a parent to young children. I will always remember that day.

But the days and weeks that followed, in which we were preparing for our beautiful twin boys to come home, quickly began to feel somewhat wrong – for me, at least. Now was the time that we were officially allowed to get excited, but somehow, I just couldn't muster it up. I would go through the motions with Michael – picking out outfits, putting up the furniture in their bedrooms, and telling people the wonderful news. But all was not well.

I didn't know what it was, but something was blocking my excitement. I simply brushed it off as a normal part of the process; after all, with pregnancy you carry your baby around for the best part of a year and already know them even before they're born, whereas with adoption, everything is brand new. Perhaps my lack of excitement was a natural reaction to that? Michael, on the other hand, was clearly on top of the world, and I was damned if I was going to spoil that for him, so I kept my mouth shut and carried on the pretence of complete elation.

My adoption leave from my job as a school librarian began about four weeks before we were due to bring the boys home. My last day at work was on an Inset day and we were receiving some training in the school hall. The headteacher announced to everybody that my colleague and I were both starting our adoption leave that day. They made a real fuss of us, with everybody asking questions and giving out hugs.

But I didn't feel right all day. I assumed I was coming down with something and put it down to the fact that I was winding down from work to begin life with my boys. But the reality was far different, and no one could have predicted it.

CHAPTER 6

Time to Say Goodbye

As the weeks passed, I started to feel worse, physically, rather than better. We began to have introductions with the twins at their foster carer's house in preparation for them coming home with us.

That first meeting was a strange experience. It was as though we were in a fish tank, being watched by the social workers and the foster carer as we met the boys at last. They were utterly gorgeous, of that there was no doubt, and I would have bundled them straight up for cuddles if they had been a friend's babies. But they weren't. They were soon to be ours.

I felt like we were expected to cry and wrap our arms around them as we began our happily ever after. But real life isn't like that. We were nervous, for a start, and knew it would be a slow process as the boys got used to us and we to them – and we were just as wary of them as they clearly were of us!

Their faces were suspicious yet expectant as they looked to me to take care of them. The only person in the world who they knew and trusted completely was their foster carer, and so the aim of the introductions was to try to lessen their attachment to her and develop a bond between them and us. In the world of adoption, it is said to be a good thing if the child has a strong attachment to their foster carer as it means it's highly likely they'll be able to replicate this attachment with the adoptive parents. But that didn't make it any easier during those early days, when they would cry for her whenever we went to pick them up.

That first day I tried to put on a front, and pretended to be overjoyed under the watchful eyes of the foster carer and social workers. In reality, I didn't feel anything – and I hated myself for it. It wasn't their fault – Lord knows it wasn't their fault. The boys had done nothing to deserve this, to deserve me in my current state. They had already been through so much in their short, sweet lives and I should have been exclusively theirs, solely existing to look after them. But I just wasn't, and I couldn't understand why.

'Why doesn't Mummy have a go at feeding them their lunch?' one of the social workers suggested as the morning drifted on. It took me a few seconds to realise she was talking about me – it just seemed so wrong, so forced.

'Do Mummy and Daddy want to read to the boys?' the foster carer asked later. It all seemed false, like we were playing a part. I suppose we were, in a way.

Michael fell in love with the boys almost straightaway after that first visit, as I knew he would. He has such a big heart and was ready to devote it entirely to them. He had photographs taken with his boys, but I just felt so separate from it all. It was as though I was looking in on someone else's family.

I was exhausted, had no energy, and couldn't muster any enthusiasm for anything. I dreaded the days we were to spend at the foster carer's house because I knew I'd be expected to hold the boys, change their nappies, play with them and feed them. I felt like my every move was being scrutinised. Any minute, I'd be found out as someone who wasn't fit not only to be *their* mum, but a mum full stop.

When you have a baby via the natural route, you have the luxury of learning to care for that baby little by little, in the privacy of your own home. With adoption introductions, you are thrown in at the deep end and need to be taught the child or children's routine by the foster carer, who has looked after them up until that point (in our case, she had cared for the boys since birth). I was so terrified of doing something wrong that I was all fingers and thumbs when changing a nappy or getting one of the boys dressed. The foster carer seemed superhuman in comparison – she baked her own bread, cooked everything from scratch, and had the knack of being able to settle each of the boys immediately if they became upset. As well as straightforward fostering, she also offered a home to underage mums who were struggling, whereby she would teach them the basics of parenting and try to encourage a bond to develop between mother and baby. I rather felt as though she saw me in the same way sometimes – as a young girl struggling with the practicalities of parenting, rather than a 29-year-old woman who was adopting with her husband.

I now recognise these feelings to be totally unfair – she was an amazing foster carer, and it was my own hang-ups that were making me feel this way towards her. But, at the time, it felt as though we were taking parenting classes as well as trying to get to know our children, and it was all just too much on top of my mystery illness.

The first day we had the twins come to our house sticks in my mind as an exceptionally low point. The plan was that the foster carer would come over to our house with them in the morning, where we would give them lunch and settle them for their nap and then take them back in the afternoon. While Michael was out of the room making a drink, one of the twins started to cry, so I picked him up and tried to comfort him. Knowing the foster carer was watching made me feel nervous and awkward, and the baby must have sensed this because he became more and more distressed. After a minute or two, the foster carer came over and took him out of my arms, saying, 'I'll take him because he's really quite distressed now,' and proceeded to calm him down almost straightaway.

She was absolutely right to do so and was in no way trying to disrespect me, but I'll never forget that feeling. I felt like a little girl who had been told off ... and I was devastated. The little confidence I had left was completely wiped out in that moment. I felt hopeless; I was never going to be like a proper mum to the boys, not like she was. Worse still, I was convinced that they themselves would see through me as well and would know I couldn't look after them properly. How could they have confidence in me as their mum when I had none in myself?

That day I felt especially dreadful, and had been physically sick throughout the morning. Michael had phoned the foster carer and asked what we should do. She said that we should still come over, because we needed to stick to the strict schedule of carefully planned meetings with the boys that the social workers had decided on. As irrational as it now sounds, I hated her for saying this. I didn't want to see her – I didn't want to see the boys.

I hated myself for that thought. I just wanted to curl up in my own bed and shut the world out. Those darling boys were the innocents in this situation. What kind of monster would want to reject them like this?

The next day I was ill again, so Michael went to visit the boys on his own. I'd pretty much refused to go. I could see that he was sad about it. He had already fallen for them in a big way and he wanted to share that with me, but I had closed myself off. He didn't know what to say for the best; anything he did say was wrong, and we would just end up arguing. I could also tell that he was as worried as hell about what was going to happen.

Something had to give.

The twins finally came home with us in February 2015. That whole day felt quite surreal; we drove to pick the boys up from the foster carer's, had some photographs taken with her and her family to go in the boys' memory boxes, then drove home with them.

Pulling into our street with them in the car felt strange and a bit awkward – what would the neighbours make of it all? With a pregnancy, you either announce it or you wait until it's so obvious there could be no doubt. With adoption, you never quite dare tell the world what's happening in case something goes wrong at the last minute (and it does happen; it's happened to people I know) and the adoption falls through. So we'd not actually told many of our neighbours by the time we brought the twins home.

Bringing them into the house was strange too. The boys didn't seem to fit into the home we'd carefully carved out over the years; they seemed at odds with all our familiar furniture and possessions, as though the two didn't quite marry up. "Incongruous" and "out of place" were the phrases that sprang to mind. They still felt like strangers, and we must have seemed that way to them, too. I did my best to make them feel at home, played with them, cuddled them, never left their side ... but it was clear from the confusion in their eyes that they were missing their foster carer, which made me sad. I was never going to compare to her in their eyes, so what was the point in trying? The boys would hate me for taking them away from her later in life, I was sure of it. They would particularly hate me since I was the female carer, and they would adore Michael as he would be the only dad they had ever known. They'd had so much upheaval and change in such short lives ...

That first day was the day I'd been dreading most of all. These tiny little people were now my responsibility. Michael would soon be going back to work, and I would be left at home with them on my own, day in, day out. How would I cope? I couldn't even cope with Michael there!

He was starting to lose patience, and we had many rows in the few days that followed (although not in front of the boys). The babies would be awake for the entire night, clearly unsettled by their new surroundings and these relative strangers who called themselves Mummy and Daddy. Michael would shout at me to get up and help him, but I didn't even have the energy to shout back, let alone to try to defend my lack of contribution, which just annoyed him more. We were both beyond tired, and I did my best to help care for the boys, but the reality was that it was mostly left to Michael, who was as terrified as I was as to what would happen on his return to work. He would constantly tell me to pull myself together, and I didn't blame him. But, no matter how hard I tried, I just couldn't seem to stir myself to be that hands-on parent I'd always wanted to be.

Our lives had done a complete U-turn within the space of only a few days. Caring for the boys was a round-the-clock job – it was essentially like having two newborns. We needed to get them used to us being their primary carers now, so there was lots of hands-on bonding with massages, cuddles, stories, and bottle-feeding. In the adoption world, the term for this type of bonding is "re-parenting" because the adoptive parents sometimes need to take the children back to their early days in the world and parent them as if they were tiny babies again in order to help the parent–child attachment to develop. We also had to be the only people to hold them for a while so as to give the boys the chance to bond with us and not cause any confusion as to who exactly "Mum" and "Dad" were. The only problem was that the bonding part wasn't actually happening – at least, not for me. It all just felt like I was going through the motions, as though bonding activities were just something else to add to the never-ending to-do list.

After a few days, the boys met our parents. Hearing my own voice referring to them as "Nana" and "Grandad" felt so wrong. I knew I was living a lie. I could tell that my mum and dad were cautious; they didn't know quite what they were allowed to do and what they weren't in terms of picking the boys up and playing with them, as we had given them so many different instructions prior to the meeting, on the advice of the social workers.

Looking back, I realise we had flooded them with too much information too quickly. 'Pick them up. Don't pick them up. Never ask us about "their story" as we won't tell you anything – it's their story to tell if they want to, not ours.'

Having said that, all of the grandparents were truly accepting of the boys as their grandchildren; being adopted didn't make them any less a part of the family in any of their eyes. We had spent months preparing them, giving them books to read on the topic and answering their questions, so by the time they met them for the first time, they were just ready to welcome them into the family with open arms.

Big Granny told me that one of her friends had said, 'How wonderful, Jean, you're going to have two new adopted grandchildren.'

She had responded, 'No, I'm going to have two new *grand-children.*'

To me, this just summed up the warmth and openness of our amazing families. In a way, that made me feel even worse about not being able to bond with my sons. I was so fortunate to have all this amazing support around me that lots of people don't have, and here I was ruining the whole experience for everyone who was so excited for us.

A few days after the boys arrived home, Michael and I had yet another argument about my lack of energy and reluctance to do anything for the boys. I even found taking them for a walk exhausting, but I took them with me when I stormed out of the house. I drove to Jen's house as I knew she was dying to meet our new arrivals. My best friend's daughter was roughly the same age as the twins and, as I put them down on her playmat, my heart sank into my shoes as I realised just how behind they were developmentally compared to her. This was partly due to the lack of care they'd received in utero and the fact that they had been born seven weeks early, but they were unable to even sit up unaided, whereas Jen's daughter was already walking.

We clearly had years of struggles and possible hospital appointments ahead of us. How was this going to be possible if I never stopped feeling as ill as I did? By now, I was starting to think I could have something seriously wrong with me – maybe the start of a chronic illness, or a severe viral infection that I might never properly recover from. I wasn't scared of being ill, but rather the idea of being ill and having the boys to take care of as well. I just wanted to feel like me again.

*

The twins both fell asleep in the car once we'd left Jen's. Rather than go straight home, I decided to just drive. Anywhere. For as long as I could. I thought I could maybe get a bit of "me" back while they were asleep; I could be someone else other than this overwhelming persona of "Mummy" that everyone expected me to be. I put the radio on and listened to a song I liked for the first time in days. But I felt disconnected from it. I was unable to relate to the words like I usually would, and had no desire to sing along.

This is life from now on, I thought.

Even now, when I drive those roads, that feeling rushes back to me all of a sudden, like a blast of cold air taking my breath away and suffocating me.

Things came to a head the next morning. I felt worse than ever – I was being sick and could hardly get out of bed. Michael insisted that I go to the doctors and that he was coming with me. I didn't put up a fight. Mum came over to watch the twins and off we went.

Sitting in the waiting room, I looked around and saw another mum who was around my age, with a tiny baby in a car seat. She looked so happy and content.

That's how I should be feeling, I thought.

Fear washed over me in sickening waves, making me feel hot and anxious. If it was true and I was seriously ill, I would never be able to have that kind of relationship with my babies. All I could picture was hard years ahead, with me struggling to even pick the boys up or meet their basic needs in between my nausea and crippling tiredness.

My doctor had been with us for the whole infertility and adoption journey so far. I kept having to run over to the little sink in his office to be sick in between trying to explain to him how I felt – exhausted, anxious, nauseous – and about how my symptoms seemed to get strangely worse every time one of the twins started crying. The doctor took some blood and urine from me and left the room without really saying anything.

The minutes ticked by while Michael and I sat there almost in silence. We didn't know what he was testing for, but it made me genuinely worried that it was a serious illness. But much to my amazement, the doctor was smiling when he eventually returned.

'I do believe the medical term is "you're pregnant",' he announced. 'About eight weeks, I think.'

I stared at him.

Michael stared at him.

It seemed like a lifetime passed in which I tried to take in the words he was saying. I had heard his words, but they didn't make sense in my head. No matter how many times I repeated them to myself, I just couldn't compute them.

'I can't be.'

'Why not?'

'Because we've just adopted twins.'

The GP knew this, of course, and was very understanding. The doctor purposely hadn't told us he was doing a pregnancy test because he hadn't wanted to raise our hopes. He gently suggested we might need to re-think the adoption in light of the news, but it wasn't that simple.

'They're not taking the babies away from us,' I said firmly, believing I would fall in love with them over time, just as Michael had done.

'Nobody's trying to,' the doctor reassured me. 'It's just something to think about.' He organised an early pregnancy scan for us on compassionate grounds, then we finally left. We must have been with him for about 45 minutes and the waiting room was now full of people staring at us as we walked by, but it didn't really register with me at all. Michael was laughing and crying at the same time as we walked back to the car. I was numb.

Neither of us spoke until we got back home – we were both in our own private world of shock.

'I'm pregnant,' I blurted out to my mum as soon as she opened the door.

Mum smiled. 'I thought you might be,' she replied, and hugged me. I stayed limp in her arms, too tired and confused to even hug her back. *Was this even good news?*

The next person I told was Jen. She was so calm and down-to-earth about it that it helped calm me down a little too. 'You've done bloody well to get to eight weeks without realising.' Jen can always find the light side of a situation, no matter what.

I then phoned our social worker and told her the news.

'I'll be straight over,' she said.

While we were waiting for the social worker to arrive, I sent Michael out to buy a pregnancy test.

'Get the most expensive one,' I told him. I somehow didn't believe the doctor's test – I'm not sure why, of course, since it would be more accurate than any shop-bought one.

The social worker laughed when I told her this, but I couldn't see anything to laugh about that day.

'If it's a case of money or the size of your house, there are things we can do for you,' she told us.

'That's not it at all. We're just worried that we won't be able to give the boys the extra care and attention they're going to need.

And how can I be a good mum to them if I carry on feeling as poorly as this?'

We knew we had to make the decision as quickly as possible – it wasn't fair to keep them for the short term if we couldn't for the long; they had been messed around too much already. The main factor behind our decision was that we would never be able to provide the special care that the twins needed and deserved while also dealing with a pregnancy and then a newborn. They deserved a family that could devote everything to them.

Michael turned to me when the social worker had left.

'Honestly,' he said, 'do you think you can cope with three children under 18 months – two with additional needs? Because it will be you doing the bulk of it when I go back to work.'

I shook my head slowly. I couldn't say the word out loud because that would make it too real. But the truth was I knew I couldn't. Maybe I could have if I was a stronger person, if I was Amanda who just takes everything in her stride ... but I only know how to be me.

*

It wasn't an easy decision to make, but it was a clear-cut one.

Michael was understandably straightforward about it.

'We need to let the social workers know sooner rather than later,' he said.

'Yes,' I agreed. 'They've had enough upheaval already. We need to do what's best for them now, not what's best for us.'

My heart was pounding as I dialled the social worker's number and waited for her to answer. When she did, I was hesitant.

'I don't think that we're going to be able to keep the twins.'

'I had a feeling you were going to say that,' came the reply. But it wasn't accusatory or harsh; it was gentle and understanding. And I was so thankful for that. If it had been otherwise, I might just have broken there and then.

That night, our social worker came with a colleague to take them back to the foster carer's. Time moved in a stilted, unfocused kind of slow motion. The things that I was hearing and seeing seemed out of sequence and unnatural, like a movie on a damaged reel, and I could scarcely take them in. I was vaguely aware of Mum and Lizzie being there, although I couldn't remember when they had arrived or whether I'd asked them to come. All I knew was that I was glad they were there.

'Do you want some time alone with them?' The social workers asked. 'Or would it be easier if we just took them now?'

'Take them now,' I replied, straightaway. Selfishly, I just wanted it to be over. I couldn't handle the shame I felt every time I looked at them.

Michael sobbed as though in pain when he cuddled the boys to him for the last time. I felt horrendous guilt course through me. This was my fault. I was the pregnant one, not Michael. I felt so ashamed.

I finally felt a spark of emotion as I kissed the boys for the last time. I squeezed them to my chest and took in the smell of their hair – the smell of them – and I held them like I would never let go. At that point, I realised I did love them – I loved them so, so much. They were my little boys, my darlings, my angels. How could I let them go and ever be quite the same person I was before? There would always be two boy-shaped holes in my heart that could never be filled. I wanted to scream out that I'd changed my mind, that this was all a mistake. But, even in that moment, I knew I had to do what was right for them. And what was right for them wasn't me.

'I will never, ever, forget you,' I whispered to each of them, kissing their foreheads.

The social workers were crying. My mum was crying. Lizzie was crying. The only people that weren't crying were the boys themselves, because they had no understanding of what was happening. But Michael and I cried enough for them.

My unknown pregnancy had just stopped me from realising it until now, had masked my true emotions. Call it hormones or whatever you will, but something had been blocking my true feelings for them. As Michael and I stood and cried at the door, watching them go, something in my heart broke clean in two.

We both sobbed ourselves to sleep that night. It was the end. It was the beginning.

CHAPTER 7

Further Adjustments

The night the twins left, I realised I couldn't face being in the house with all their things around me. It looked as though the house had been frozen in time – all around were the remnants of the two little lives that had intertwined with ours so briefly: half-drunk bottles of milk still stood on the table, tiny vests were drying on the clothes horse, and the toys they had been playing with still littered the floor. It felt like some kind of macabre museum, an homage to what might have been.

I stayed over at Mum and Dad's that night while Michael stayed at home. I asked him to come and stay with me, thinking we would face everything together the next day, but he wanted to stay in his own familiar surroundings and I respected that.

'Mum's offered for me to go and stay with her and Dad tonight,' I told him. 'I just can't face being here with all the boys' things. You can come as well if you like.'

'No, I'm going to stay here if that's okay with you,' he replied, without hesitation. 'I just want to be in my own space tonight.'

'Of course.'

The great thing about being with the same person each and every day for years is that you get to know each other to the very core; I just *knew* by looking at him that this was genuinely his reason for not coming with me. I suppose we all have our different ways of coping, and in hindsight I realise we probably needed that time apart in order to try to process things in our own ways.

I barely slept that night. If I *did* drop off to sleep, I would jolt awake minutes later, thinking that perhaps it had all been one long, confusing dream: the adoption, the pregnancy, the boys being taken away. I kept laying my hand across my tummy – I just couldn't believe there really was a baby inside. After all the months and years of longing for a child, a miracle had happened – and I didn't know how to feel about it. For one fleeting moment in time, for less than a day, we had had three children after pining even for one.

*

The next day, I knew I had to start thinking practically. Although I could have happily stayed at Mum and Dad's for the foreseeable, I knew I couldn't leave Michael at home on his own when he, too, was confused and upset. This was the time when we needed to stand strong and work together to try to see a way forward.

The first thing I did was ask my sister to come over and help us clean the house. The events of the previous day meant that the place was a veritable midden, and I needed to get the twins' things packed away in order to maintain any kind of sanity. It wasn't that I wanted them gone and forgotten; more that it was too painful to sit looking at it all when we knew that they were gone and wouldn't be coming back.

I felt remorse, yes, a deep, deep sadness that we had had our beautiful sons in our lives for a brief moment before they were gone, more fleetingly than snowflakes melting into puddles. Then there was the guilt: our two tiny angels had once again been cast adrift by those who were supposed to protect them above all others. But I also felt relief that I wouldn't have to deal with the responsibility of being a mum to two little boys who were going to need constant, specialist parental care for at least the next few years. The relief turned to guilt, which turned to remorse, and so it went on.

Michael and I went through dozens of these vicious cycles during the early days after the twins' departure. It was almost like everything that had happened was too big to process all in one go, so we would feel the joy of the pregnancy, followed a split-second later by the memory of the night the twins left, which made us feel horrendous guilt, and in turn made us wonder whether we had done the right thing. And we were never at the same point in the cycle as each other, so our emotions often conflicted with those of the other person. All this meant that we both just became more and more confused and at odds with each other.

The day after their departure, we put everything that belonged to the boys to one side to be collected by the social worker. Everything that had been bought for them, either by us or as gifts from family and friends, was sent to them – it just wouldn't have felt right to keep any of it; it had been bought especially for the twins and they were to have it all.

It also felt important and necessary for us to return our living room to the way it had been before the twins arrived. Furniture that had been pushed against the walls to make a large space for playing in was duly moved quietly and unceremoniously back to the centre of the room. I felt strongly that we needed to have some time back as a couple for a while before starting to focus on the new baby, as we hadn't been just "Ali and Michael" since before we'd got married. It was like there'd always been something to test us; we'd had the infertility, the adoption process, approvals, and now this. Part of that included not having everything be child-friendly. When the time was right, we would think about it again and make the necessary alterations to prepare for our new arrival, but the time wasn't right just yet.

The next thing we needed to do was to let people know what had happened. I felt so ashamed, as though people would think we'd just sent the twins packing as soon as a "better offer"– the possibility of a biological child of our own – had come along. I felt fickle and foolish, like a child who discards a toy as soon as they see a new one. I imagined that everybody would despise me. We'd spent so many months preparing everyone for the twins' arrival; everybody was excited to meet them and proud of us for going through the tough process, and now here we were saying the deal was off.

I asked Jen to let the rest of my friends know as I couldn't bear the thought of their disappointment in me. Later, when they had all sent messages of total and unconditional support and love, I messaged them:

Thank you for not hating me.

How the hell could we hate you? came Nicole's prompt reply.

I felt so humble and undeserving, but I also felt a huge wave of relief. I don't think I'd have been able to face the rest of the world without the support of my best friends!

To my surprise, I found that everyone we told shared their attitude – nobody was anything but supportive.

Later that week, I phoned work to let them know. I knew that I'd need to go back to work sooner rather than later as I would soon be finishing again – this time on maternity leave. The headteacher arranged for me to go in and see her the following week. It was a difficult meeting. I cried as I re-lived what had happened, right up to the twins being taken away. But the head was so kind to me and, as I left, she turned to me and said, 'Now don't you feel guilty about anything. That little baby in there will pick up on all your feelings, so you need to be strong.'

Something clicked within me at her words, and the cloud of shame began to lift a little. The last thing I wanted was for my unborn baby to sense any negativity from me! I had seen firsthand the long-lasting impact that negativity can have on a baby during pregnancy, so knew I couldn't inflict this on yet another young life; there are enough of them suffering out there as it is. When I relayed all this to Michael, he seemed relieved – relieved that I was, in a way, giving us both permission to finally feel good about the pregnancy.

Before my return to work, the day of the early pregnancy scan arrived. I think Michael and I both felt out of place as we sat in the waiting room with all the other expectant parents. We had already closed the doors to biological children in order to go down our chosen path of adoption, and yet we'd now been thrown into this alien world. We felt like intruders.

It struck me was that it was a non-negotiable prerequisite of adoption that prospective parents have to be non-smokers, and yet here we were, looking at posters telling pregnant mothers not to smoke. There seemed to be a strange irony in that. Adopters are specialist parents who are put through a hell of a lot to even be considered – only the best of the best will actually be approved – and yet birth mothers, who have the absolute privilege of being able to carry a beautiful baby, have to be told not to smoke while pregnant? How was that fair, or just, or right?

Right up until the moment we saw our baby's heart beating on the monitor, I still thought deep down that the whole thing was a mistake. I expected nothing to show up on the scan; I was sure that my womb would be just as empty as it had always been.

'Well, there's definitely a baby there,' the sonographer informed us. 'It's a very tiny baby, only as big as a baked bean, but it's there.'

I looked up at the screen, feeling as though I was being shown a video of another woman's baby. I thought it was all a big trick – surely that couldn't be *my* scan up there? But I had to believe that it was true. What other choice was there?

I turned to Michael and saw tears of happiness in his eyes. I know him through and through, and knew that he was smitten for sure, that this baby and I were his whole world from then on. Right then and there on that hospital bed, I knew that I had to do everything I could to look after this little baked bean who had fought and clawed its way into our lives against all the odds. It had given its all to make sure it implanted itself firmly into that uterus wall, and the least I could do was to love and nurture it from now on.

*

A few days later, I returned to work. I had asked the headteacher to let the rest of the staff know before I arrived at school and to ask them to please not ask me about the twins yet. I was finding it hard enough just thinking about them, so I felt like I might break into a million pieces if someone asked me questions.

As it happened, everyone at work was brilliant and really supportive, far more so than I could have hoped for or deserved. There were no negative comments at all, although I could have completely understood if there had been. My friend and colleague who had adopted at the same time as me was particularly amazing about it, which blew me away – I wouldn't have blamed her if she had never wanted to speak to me again. We had been through the whole process together, shared things with each other that I wouldn't have even shared with my family, and now I felt as though I was somehow betraying her. As though I was saying that, now that I was pregnant, my adopted children were no longer good enough for me and, by default, her child wasn't good enough either.

I was nervous to see the colleague who had been hired to cover my adoption leave, which was intended to be for 12 months, but I need not have worried. The first thing she did when she saw me was to give me a hug and tell me it was okay. In the end, all my fretting had been for nothing!

Unfortunately, Michael did receive a couple of negative comments when he returned to work. He came home upset one evening because somebody had asked whether the baby was his, probably seeing it as a bit of banter, but the timing was completely wrong; everything was still too raw. Another colleague had commented that he didn't know how we could just give up two children like that. Michael's reply was to tell him to walk a mile in his shoes, but I could still tell he was distressed by these comments and I hated that. He has since admitted that the comments made him feel even worse about our decision than he did already and made him question whether we had done the right thing. Although I was still having those same doubts myself, I could only reassure him that we had – we'd not only done the right thing for us, but also for the new baby and the twins.

I knew that we could never reverse the decision that we had made, that we would always now have to live with what we had done. There was no going back. It was done. But nevertheless, I would still ask Michael the same thing every day: 'Did we do the right thing?'

'We couldn't have done anything else,' would come the reply.

I know he wished I would stop asking him, stop going round and round in the same tired circles. I also know he was telling me what he knew I needed to hear, to protect me, even though he was asking those same questions of himself. We were both torturing ourselves about it, but the difference was that Michael mostly kept his feelings to himself, whereas I needed to constantly vocalise and question it. He does that mostly to protect me from what he's feeling, and that's something I'm still to this day trying to work on – getting him to open up more to me. He needs to be cared for just as much as I do, if only he'd let me do it.

Now was the time we needed to stick together more than ever, to stand united as a couple. But that's not always easy when you're each in your own world of pain.

CHAPTER 8

The World Shifts Again

Getting used to being pregnant was a strange experience. I would constantly forget about it in the early days and then have jolting moments of realisation as everything that had happened came flooding back. I think I was largely in shock. Perhaps forgetting everything – the infertility, the adoption, the pregnancy – was my brain's way of coping? But ultimately you can't hide from it for more than a few hours at a time when a new life is growing inside you.

I continued to feel nauseous up until about 10 weeks in, and the tiniest of things could start me vomiting, from the sight of a loose hair in the bathroom sink, to the woody smell of our new wardrobes. I also had an overwhelming feeling of having been "switched off", as though someone had flicked off a switch on my back or taken out my batteries, but I gather this is quite common. I was fortunate, though, not to experience any negative reactions to food. I could eat what I liked (although my only experience of cravings was the day I just couldn't stop eating celery).

These physical symptoms started to fade with the passage of time and I gradually began to feel well. I loved the sight of my growing bump and relished all those moments I had thought would never happen, like my first appointment with the midwife and feeling the first kick. I loved having the opportunity to share my pregnancy with Amanda and Nicole, who were also pregnant. (Nicole was due seven days after me, Amanda a few weeks before.) They had both shared their happy news as soon as they found out about my pregnancy, in a way so that I would know I wouldn't be going through it alone, I think. This had been a strange kind of comfort to me; two of my best friends sharing my experience and having their maternity leave at the same time as me.

Having said this, I still had an underlying feeling of detachment from the baby bubbling away within me, as though it was someone else's child that I was just taking care of for nine months.

The first time we heard the baby's heartbeat, for example, Michael and my midwife were both grinning like Cheshire cats, clearly overjoyed that everything sounded healthy and as it should be. They were looking at me expectantly, as though waiting for my jubilant reaction. To me, however, it was just a pleasant sound, one which made me smile but didn't seem particularly pivotal to me. The midwife encouraged me to make a recording on my phone, which hadn't even occurred to me – why would I want to record a "pleasant sound"? If I wasn't particularly moved by it, surely no one else would be?

The first appointment with my midwife particularly sticks in my mind. She ran through the standard list of questions with me, ticking each box as I answered. Then came the question:

'Was this pregnancy planned?'

I looked at Michael and knew I had to answer "no", but the word stuck in my throat. All she really wanted to know was whether or not I'd been taking my folic acid and vitamin D, eating properly and abstaining from alcohol. But the word just wouldn't come. Never before had a baby been so planned and yet so unplanned. In the end, Michael had to answer for me.

Quite late on in my pregnancy, at around six months, I started to feel a little unwell again. I was at work one afternoon when one part of my lower back started to feel itchy. I also felt a bit shivery and delicate, as though I couldn't bear anything touching me, even my clothes. I was working late and was in a presentation when I decided I couldn't bear it any longer. Luckily, I was sitting at the back of the room, so I hoiked my top up at the back to scratch the itch and felt a really strange, smooth kind of rash there, not like anything I'd had before. When I got home, I looked my symptoms up on the NHS site and suspected I had shingles. I started to panic straightaway, as I knew chickenpox can harm the unborn baby and assumed shingles could too. I phoned the doctors and was told to come in straightaway, and half an hour later I had my shingles diagnosis. Luckily, shingles, unlike chickenpox, has no ill-effect on the baby, so I was able to carry on as normal.

It was at about the same time I found I had shingles that my problems with sleep started. I had always been a great sleeper up until that point, so lying awake for hours on end was alien to me when it started to happen. I couldn't put my finger on it at first; I wasn't hugely uncomfortable in my pregnancy and the shingles weren't so painful that they should affect my sleep – but nevertheless, there I was, wide-eyed and wired for large parts of most nights while Michael snored gently beside me. And oh, how I hated him for it! Why should he have been able to fall asleep at the drop of a hat when I couldn't? I realise now that it was the feelings of guilt over the failed adoption that were starting to resurface particularly strongly as the birth came near, but at the time I was at my wits' end. I once read a book from cover to cover in one night, in the desperate hope that it might make me sleepy. (In my experience, a book had never failed to entice me into sleep.) All my old tried and tested methods of falling asleep were failing me when I really needed them. Suddenly, everything I had taken for granted was now thrown into doubt.

The insomnia was starting to take its toll on my work and other aspects of my life, and I knew I'd need to be as rested as possible for when the baby came along. And so after much coercion from Michael, I visited the GP at about seven months pregnant to see if I could be given anything, even something herbal, to help with my sleep.

Unfortunately, the doctor I saw was not my usual GP (the lovely one who had told me I was pregnant). He hadn't been available. I explained, little by little, to the new doctor about not being able to sleep and being haunted by my thoughts at night, but all I seemed to do was anger him.

'Why have you come to me today? Do you honestly expect me to give you something to help you sleep while you're pregnant?'

The words "you stupid girl" rang in my head. He might not have actually said it, but I could tell that that was how he'd wanted to finish his sentence. In my embarrassment, and because my emotions were heightened due to the sleep deprivation, I started to cry, but this only spurred him on more.

'Why are you crying?' he snapped.

His conduct during this appointment sparked a wariness of medical professionals. It was easier for me to try to keep things hidden and try to deal with them myself since I didn't know which doctors I could trust. The irony was that whenever I saw this doctor with Michael present, he couldn't have been more helpful – the only issue was the fact that he always addressed Michael instead of me, even though it was *my* appointment, *my* health problem. But when I was on my own? It was a completely different story. Did he not like women? Or was it just me? I don't suppose I'll ever know for sure. I know I wasn't imagining it because Michael noticed it too, and said so. We were both shocked to find such blatant sexism going on in this day and age, in this country. I didn't want to speak out about it at the time as I was already feeling vulnerable and weak, but I sure as hell would if it happened now. Ladies, we are worth so much more than that!

In spite of everything, there were some lovely parts to my pregnancy too.

One happy memory in particular was a trip to the *Coronation Street* set to celebrate Nicole's birthday. As a group, we had decided to each be a different character from "the Street" for the day and we rocked up at Nicole's house wearing our respective masks. At the wheel of the car was Amanda wearing a Steve McDonald mask, and next to her was Heather, who had come as Norris Cole. The tears streamed down my face as I saw Steve and Norris peering out through the windscreen! The car had also been given its own makeover and was now a Street Cars taxi. In moments like those, when I felt I might burst from laughing, I knew somehow that everything would come out alright again in the end.

Michael and I found out we were having a boy at my 20-week scan. I already somehow knew that we were – I have always just known I would have boys; that's why it was the natural route to go down when being matched with the twins. The scan really just confirmed what we already knew, and it was a relief; getting used to the idea of having a girl would have just been something else to have to adapt to. We quickly narrowed our name choices down to Jacob or Henry – they weren't family names, just names that we both liked.

I would often sit quietly and just enjoy the sensation of his kicks. I was scared to death about how I would cope when the baby arrived, but he was our little miracle and he was letting me know he was there and that I needed to look after myself as best I could for him.

There were also times when I did manage a good night's sleep, and for the days that followed those nights would give me a real boost. At times I felt so healthy that I almost forgot about sleep altogether. But it would always be there, waiting round the next corner, to trip me up again.

During my third trimester, I was found to be a carrier of Group B Strep, a type of streptococcal bacteria. This is a very common bacteria that two in five people carry. It's not usually a problem and people can go their whole lives without knowing they have it, but it needs to be addressed during pregnancy as it can be very harmful if passed to the baby. Unfortunately, Group B Strep is not routinely tested for in the UK and was only detected in my case when I was tested for a water infection. This meant that I would need to receive intravenous antibiotics during my birth, for which I would now need to be in the consultant-led unit of the maternity hospital, rather than the more relaxed midwife-led one.

Once again, I felt disappointed in myself; my body was throwing me curve balls left, right, and centre, and there was nothing I could do about it. I had been prepared to have my baby on the midwife-led unit and now the plans were changing again. I knew that the experience would be very different – there would be no opportunity for the birthing chair that I'd had in mind, no option for the birthing pool. Nobody else I knew had had Group B Strep, so why me? I worried that I would go into sudden labour and that there wouldn't be time to administer the antibiotics the baby would need. I worried that I wouldn't be listened to and that the antibiotics wouldn't materialise. Everything seemed so far out of my control; I was at the mercy of the professionals and wasn't sure I even trusted them. But I had to.

Despite my insomnia, time passed as it tends to do and my pregnancy neared its end. About a week before our son was born, Michael and I were watching *Strictly Come Dancing* one evening when I realised I hadn't felt the baby move much at all that day. This was strange, as he was usually very active. Trying not to panic Michael, I phoned the hospital and they told me to come in. Fortunately, once we'd arrived and I was hooked up to the monitor, it turned out that everything was fine, but it served as a reminder that this life inside of me was so delicate and could be so easily harmed. After all we'd been through, I was determined to deliver him safely into the world!

As much as I would have loved to experience a natural labour and the excitement of the early-morning dash to the hospital, it wasn't to be. I was booked in for an induction two weeks after my due date, on 15th October 2015. Knowing that my baby boy was soon to be placed in my arms, I tried to get as much sleep as I could beforehand, often napping throughout the day. But this, of course, made my night-time sleep even worse. By the time the morning of the 15th dawned, I was already horribly sleep-deprived, but I tried to put it to the back of my mind.

There was no turning back now.

CHAPTER 9

Drugs, Sweets, and a Brand-New Person

The morning of the 15th October 2015 dawned sunny and clear, but there was the noticeable bite of winter starting to drift in on the air. As we drove towards the hospital, I felt a mixture of emotions course through me. I was happy of course, and excited. But where I think I differed from most first-time mums is that, rather than feeling nervous and scared about the actual process of giving birth, I felt nervous and scared that my last night as a childless woman had produced very little sleep. *When would I next get the chance for an uninterrupted slumber?* I wondered.

I pushed these thoughts away as we entered the maternity assessment unit, where I was to be induced. I was shown to a small ward with two other ladies on it, both of whom had been started off the previous night but were not yet in active labour.

At about eleven o'clock in the morning, I was called into a small clinic where I had a pessary inserted. I winced and tried to struggle away as the procedure was carried out, and it was at this point that I felt my first pangs of nerves about the delivery – if I couldn't bear the pessary going in, how on earth was I to endure hours of agonising labour?

After the procedure had been completed, I was shown back to my bed. Michael went to find us some lunch and returned a short while later with sandwiches and magazines for me. The nurses had told us that there could be quite a wait before anything happened, and that I may well need an injection in addition to the pessary to really get things going.

I ate my sandwiches and settled down to read the magazines, starting to feel as though maybe this wouldn't be so bad after all; I could relax and chill out and perhaps even get a couple of hours' kip before anything happened.

How wrong I was.

Almost an hour to the minute after I'd had the pessary, I started to feel cramp-like pains in my stomach. I tried to push them out of my mind at first, but they soon started to become more intense. I gripped Michael's hand.

'This can't be right,' I said to him. 'Surely it shouldn't be hurting this much already?'

Michael went to fetch a midwife, especially as the ladies on either side of me did not appear to be in any pain – and they had started their inductions the evening before!

I wondered if the other ladies *were* feeling exactly like me, but were just able to manage their pain better. I tried and tried to stop myself from crying out – I didn't want them to hear me making a big fuss over what could be nothing!

Michael soon returned with one of the midwives, who looked me up and down very unsympathetically and gave me two paracetamol tablets.

'It won't have started that quickly,' she said dismissively.

I felt embarrassed by her words, like a child who has been admonished for doing something wrong at school. I hoped against hope that nobody else in the ward had heard her; I was clearly just making a holy show of myself in her eyes.

I knew immediately that paracetamol would not even touch the sides of my pain and within minutes I was writhing on the floor, still trying to hold in my agonised cries while Michael tried to hold me steady. My overriding thought was that I needed to be as low down and close to the floor as I could get, because it felt lovely and cool against my clammy skin. I think it's fair to say that what I was feeling wasn't even pain anymore; it transcended that. It felt as though I was losing touch with reality.

A few minutes later, Michael went to fetch a midwife again. I think I'd scared the wits out of him when he saw how much pain I was in, as I usually have quite a high tolerance to it. He recalls now an overwhelming appearance of helplessness on my face and that my eyes were wild with fear.

This time (thank the Lord), the young midwife who was despatched to care for me was the lovely one I'd seen just the week before, when I'd had concerns about reduced movement in the baby. She examined me and told me that I was two centimetres dilated. She offered me some pethidine, and I gratefully accepted it before she had even finished her sentence! I began to feel very happy and chilled out almost as soon as I'd swallowed the pills, as though I'd drunk a couple of glasses of my favourite Chardonnay.

What felt like just a couple of minutes later – but was actually a good few hours according to Michael (the pethidine had helped a lot!) – I was transferred to the room where I would be giving birth. It was spacious and comfortable, although I didn't have the luxury of being able to move around. I had to stay on the bed because I was being given the intravenous antibiotics to ensure the Strep B had no ill-effect on my baby.

Once we were settled in our room, Michael and I started to joke around, taking photographs of my compression stockings and sending them to my friends. I also sent photos of the huge amount of sweets that we'd packed; my great love of sweets is a long-standing in-joke between me and my friends, so I always get them for birthdays and Christmases.

As my labour pains slowly started to become more intense, I really started to lose track of time. I couldn't tell if we had been in there for minutes or hours waiting for our baby to arrive. There was no night and day in that room as far as I was concerned. The consultant came into the room a couple of times to check on the baby's heart rate, which was a little erratic. The midwife told us that some of the other consultants would have had us go down for a caesarean section by then, but ours appeared to be quite confident that everything was still manageable and on-course for a normal birth.

My mum arrived somewhere along the line (midnight, according to Michael). I must have started to feel a bit worse by this time because, as soon as she came into the room, I called, 'Hi, Mum!' then proceeded to throw up all over her shoes.

While the baby's heart rate didn't seem to be too much of a concern to the consultant, my blood pressure *was*. It had been raised on and off throughout the latter stages of my pregnancy, but now it was consistently high. In the end, it was decided that I would have an epidural to try to lower my blood pressure.

Between my moans the consultant explained what would happen, and then the epidural was administered. My labour was slow to progress, so I was glad of the extra help! At about five o'clock in the morning, Michael told my mum to go home. We could be there for hours longer yet and the strains of tiredness were beginning to show on her face – like me, she does not cope well without sleep.

Towards late morning I began to push, but after an hour of pushing nothing much seemed to be happening and I again heard murmurs of a caesarean. I also saw one of the doctors come towards me with a tray of gleaming instruments, including the formidable-looking forceps. Jen had had to have forceps a year earlier when she gave birth to her little girl, and all I had in my head at that moment, clear as a bell in the midst of my absolute exhaustion, was Jen's voice saying, '... and then the forceps went in, and I thought I was dying.'

I was determined that those forceps were going nowhere near me, so I pushed and pushed until I thought I was going to pass out.

The morning slipped into the afternoon in a haze of Entonox and finally, at one o'clock on the dot, our beautiful little Jacob Henry was born.

When he was born, Michael asked me whether I wanted to call him Jacob or Henry, and I just blurted out 'Jacob Henry'. It was just the first thing that came into my head. I was in no fit state to be thinking rationally – I could probably just as easily have blurted out 'Carrot'! Luckily, Michael agreed.

It felt so dream-like when he was handed to me. I looked down at him calmly as he nuzzled into my chest, and I could fathom that he was mine. Michael was sobbing with happiness, but, strangely, I just couldn't relate to these feelings at all.

CHAPTER 10

Fragments

I find it so hard to write this, but I didn't feel a connection to my son when he was born.

What I remember are fragments; parts of the hours and days that followed that fit together but somehow also don't. I remember that Jacob was crying from the shock of being so rudely thrust into the outside world. I remember that as soon as he was placed on my chest, he calmed down. I remember feeling like I was moving around in a daze, as though I was in slow motion and everything else was continuing at normal pace around me.

We were taken into another room where Jacob was weighed and dressed in his tiny first outfit, which was grey and white and said "Little Bear" on the hat. I was able to have a shower. In those few minutes, it was a relief to be away from him for even a few minutes – I instantly hated the notion that he was supposed to be an extension of me in those early days. I just wanted to be autonomous again, to be my own person.

This was so at odds with the mother I'd always thought I would be. I'd always pictured myself with my baby permanently attached to me, day and night. I was going to be a sling-wearing, breastfeeding-on-demand, skin-to-skin earth mother. That was just how it was going to be. So feeling like I wanted to be apart from Jacob so soon after his birth just confused my befuddled mind even more.

After my shower we were shown to a side room which would be our home for the next few hours at least. I needed to go to the toilet, so I left Jacob with Michael while I ensconced myself in the clinical, white bathroom with some magazines that I'd brought along to read while I was waiting for my induction to take effect. (As it happened, I had barely even glanced at them before my labour had begun in earnest.)

I felt incredibly guilty for using the bathroom as a way to be alone; I knew I was expected to be with my baby indefinitely during that time, yet here I was, taking my time and reading magazines while Jacob and Michael were left to it in the other room. As I leafed through the articles, I felt jealous of all the celebrities who were happily living their lives, smiling out from the pages at me. *Would I ever smile again?* I wondered. *Would I ever feel or look like me again?* I didn't understand how all those celebrity mums seemed to be just carrying on as normal, as though they had never even had babies. I looked on in awe at the new mums who were pictured on nights out just days after giving birth – how on earth was that socially acceptable when "ordinary" women like me had it drummed into us that we must not let our babies out of our sights? And how were they not so exhausted that it was all they could do to venture outside to put the bins out, let alone go out into town? As if we don't already put enough pressure on ourselves to be the perfect mum, we also have society's version of perfection thrust upon us as well. And then we sit in universities across the land and wonder why postnatal depression is so prevalent.

*

Once back in the room with Jacob and Michael, I tried my first breastfeed. Other than having seen friends breastfeeding, I had no clue at all what I was supposed to be doing. I put Jacob to the breast; he made some suckling movements, then, a few seconds later, his mouth slipped off again. In my fog of exhaustion, reality was skewed, and I figured that he must have fed for long enough. *Perhaps newborns only need a few seconds per feed*, I thought.

At about nine o'clock, Michael went home. We hadn't been told that he was allowed to stay with us overnight (we only found that bit out later), so I was left alone with Jacob. Each time I laid my head on the pillow to try to rest, he would squirm and cry for another feed. And so the cycle continued throughout the night; a few seconds' worth of feeding followed by two minutes' rest, followed by squirming and crying, followed by another feed. I pressed the buzzer for assistance a couple of times – once because I had passed a huge blood clot that needed to be checked (it turned out to be fine) and once to say that Jacob had passed his first stool. I had been told earlier that I must tell someone when Jacob passed his first bowel movement so it could be checked; however, the nurse that came to me said that wasn't the case and I felt a bit silly for having done so afterwards.

'Everything going alright with the breastfeeding?' she asked, as she turned to leave the room.

'Err ... yes, okay I think.'

I started to explain about the tiny feeds that only lasted for a few seconds at a time, but she had already gone. The staff were very clearly overworked and I felt guilty for bothering them. I assumed they thought that I should know what I was doing at 30 years old and should have been able to look after my baby on my own.

At about four o'clock in the morning, I called for help and told the nurse who came that I was worried I wasn't feeding Jacob properly, as he was only staying latched for a few seconds at a time. She explained that she didn't have time to show me but that she could give me a booklet on breastfeeding to read. I spent the rest of the night trying to work out what the hell I was supposed to be doing, trying to adopt the positions shown in the booklet with Jacob in my arms while being so tired I couldn't see straight. I tried several of the different positions suggested, but there was no improvement in his latch. I felt vulnerable and frightened and couldn't stop shaking. I felt like I was failing my son.

When Michael came back in the morning, I told him about my struggles with the breastfeeding. He went to fetch help and a complete angel of a healthcare assistant came in to spend some time with us. She made me feel human again for a while, talking about her family and her life outside the hospital, and she even managed to make me laugh. She told me about a time when her son had been trying to grow some tomato plants in the garage. She was convinced they needed light, so she moved them onto the kitchen windowsill and started to tend to them. All was fine until her son came home and started to panic, quickly herding his precious plants back into the garage. That was when she realised they weren't tomato plants at all, but cannabis. Up until that point, I'd imagined life had stopped outside the hospital, outside that room even, but it gave me some comfort to know that other people were indeed carrying on as normal. *Maybe there would be hope for me too one day in the future?*

Despite all the healthcare assistant's efforts over a number of hours, we had still had no joy with the feeding and we made the decision to switch to formula-feeding, hopefully as a temporary measure while I learnt to breastfeed him properly. I was heartbroken. I felt I was depriving Jacob of his basic care. Hardly anyone I knew had formula-fed and I had so badly wanted to feed the natural way. Some areas of society would have us believe that formula milk is the equivalent of pumping poison into our babies!

'Breast is best.'

'Babies should be exclusively breastfed for their first six months.'

'Breastfeeding helps achieve optimum health and development in infants.'

'Exclusive breastfeeding reduces infant mortality.'

These are just some of the messages that expectant and new mums are flooded with in those early days. While I'm sure nobody would dispute their truth, there also needs to be a balance between the promotion of breastfeeding and not making already vulnerable, exhausted mums feel demonised if they are unable to. It seems like we can't catch a break at any turn.

I was shown how to express some colostrum that was then syringed into Jacob's mouth, so at least that was some comfort. A line from the breastfeeding booklet played over and over again in my head: "Babies already know how to breastfeed. It's mothers who need to learn how to do it." I felt ashamed as I put the bottle to Jacob's lips; I had failed him at the first hurdle and was possibly putting his health and his future development in jeopardy. I was still determined that I would breastfeed in the longer term; formula-feeding had never even been on my radar throughout the pregnancy. It just wasn't the "done thing" amongst my friends. I didn't want anyone to know I wasn't breastfeeding yet, so I would try to hide the bottle whenever somebody came into the room.

All the while, visitors came and went – my parents, my sister, my auntie and uncle. I knew I had to pretend that everything was okay with me, so I went through the motions, talking about the birth and our plans for the next few days. By the time my auntie and uncle visited, I was mortified to realise that the sheets I was lying on had not yet been changed in the time I had been there. I had been told to keep clean and dry to avoid infection, yet I was sitting in heavily soiled sheets that were covered in blood and various other postpartum bodily fluids that tend to appear.

Michael and I asked for the sheets to be changed several times, but to no avail. In the end, after my auntie and uncle had left, I ended up stripping the bed myself and taking the sheets out into the corridor.

'Please,' I almost begged one of the nurses. 'Can I have clean sheets?'

Having the dirty sheets thrown at their feet meant that the staff couldn't ignore me anymore, and they went off to fetch me some clean ones. Michael and I had to put the new bedding on ourselves (despite me really being in no fit state physically to do this, having just *given birth*), but I was beyond caring by that point.

It felt wonderful to have a clean bed to lie on once again. The small things make such a big difference when feeling so vulnerable post-birth!

Although we had switched to formula-feeding, it became apparent that Jacob wasn't latching onto the bottle either. Hours went by and the lovely, patient healthcare assistant called for more help as Jacob became hungrier and hungrier. Eventually, he was examined by a doctor who said that he had such a build-up of rubbish on his chest that he wasn't able to feed properly. From then onwards, Jacob was propped up in his crib so that he could breathe more easily and hopefully start to clear the rubbish away. When Jacob took his first full feed from a bottle late in the evening, the relief was instant and immense.

By this time, we had been told that Michael was welcome to stay overnight with me, so he suggested I get some sleep while he looked after Jacob, now that he was able to be fed from a bottle. I was so relieved that Michael was going to be with me. If nothing else, at least he would be able to see the struggles I'd been having with his own eyes.

As I lay down to sleep, I heard a commotion out in the corridor. The sad and desperate voice of a young lady was screaming, 'I'm going to kill my baby!'

Michael poked his head out into the corridor and saw two doctors running towards the woman. One of the doctors injected her with something (most likely a sedative), and things quietened down immediately.

Her voice still haunts my dreams from time to time. The most frightening thing is, at that moment in time, I didn't blame her for having such an abhorrent urge. The last thing I wanted to do was hurt Jacob, but the way I was feeling, I could almost see how someone could feel that way. Once you reach that level of exhaustion, your thoughts stop being rational and any sense of reality is gone. Nothing seems real anymore, so you think it probably wouldn't matter if something awful happens. Nothing can affect someone who is numb to normal emotional responses.

*

At this point, I had gone almost 72 hours without sleep and was hallucinating badly. I was having conversations with people who weren't there.

'Your baby's lovely,' they kept saying.

'Thanks,' I would reply. 'It's a little girl, called Jacob.'

I was repeatedly referring to Jacob as "she", and genuinely believed he was a girl. I had no idea what day of the week it was, what time it was, or how long I'd been in hospital. It could have been days, it could have been months.

Michael and I both tried to tell the staff, but we were brushed off to begin with.

'Well, you won't get much sleep with a newborn,' we were told, time and time again.

'No,' I tried to tell them, 'I don't mean I'm not getting much sleep. I mean I haven't had even a minute's sleep in three days now.'

But it was to no avail. I felt desperate – here we were asking for help, only to be told there was none. I honestly couldn't see how I would ever sleep again.

Eventually, at about two o'clock in the morning, Michael insisted I see a doctor. When the doctor came, he reluctantly agreed to give me something to help me sleep, and made us promise that Michael would be in sole care of Jacob while I was under the effects of the medication.

'We have another lady on the main maternity ward,' he said. 'I gave her sleeping medication earlier on, then she tried to pick up her baby and dropped him onto the floor.'

I wondered why he was telling me this. Was he wanting me to change my mind and say I wouldn't take the pills after all? Is it really fair to expect that of someone who is suffering so acutely? While it was an awful thing to have happened, I didn't know this lady or her baby, so it was nothing to me. I wasn't capable of empathy in that moment.

I swallowed the pills gratefully, not stopping to ask any questions about what they were or any side effects. As long as they made me sleep, I didn't care.

I lay in bed, willing myself to drop off, but the pills wouldn't work. I was completely wired and hallucinating – everywhere I looked, I could see terrible, frightening faces of people who, while not there physically, absolutely were there in my head. These were the people from the horror movies, the worst of the worst nightmares. They were coming to harm me and there was nothing I could do about it. I was on constant high alert, waiting for the people in the room to either come and kill me or leave me be.

'Where is she?' I kept asking Michael.

'Who?'

'The baby.'

In my mind, Jacob was a girl, but she wasn't mine. I was supposed to be looking after her for somebody else, but why weren't they coming back for her? *Don't they know I need to sleep? I shouldn't have to be watching someone else's baby like this; they should be doing it themselves. I don't even know this baby's name, for goodness' sake!*

These hallucinations were exhausting and would not let me rest. Eventually, I did manage about three hours' sleep. I tried to see this as a positive – and, for now at least, some of the hallucinations had been staved off.

When the morning broke, Michael went home to get a few hours' rest. The nurses told me that I would be able to go home that day, so I spent some time getting my things together in anticipation. I wandered down the corridor to get some breakfast and was once again told off for leaving Jacob in the room on his own. I just couldn't see any problem with it – okay, so he might get stolen, but then at least I might be able to get some uninterrupted rest. That was how muddled my thoughts and feelings were at that time. The nurses either didn't seem to notice I was acting strangely, didn't have the time to deal with it, or just didn't care and wanted me gone so they could have my room back. I hope it was the first one.

Michael returned after lunch and we were shown how to bathe Jacob. He also had his newborn checks on his eyes, heart, hips, and testicles, which were thankfully all normal. After my three hours of sleep, I felt just about strong enough to give breastfeeding another try, and this time there was a nurse available to sit with me and show me how to do it properly. I could tell straightaway that the latch was perfect this time – it was such a unique, wonderful feeling, like nothing I have experienced before or since. It was something very primal, something instinctive. My baby and I just fitted together in that moment and for the first time since Jacob's birth, I felt some kind of a connection to him. I fed him for 45 minutes straight that afternoon. I only wish I'd known then that it would be our first and last proper feed. If I had, I would have tried to remember every small detail, every suckle, every stroke of his cheek. Most of all, I would have got Michael to take a photograph.

A lady from the local community breastfeeding team came to my room just after we had finished feeding.

'Are you breastfeeding or formula-feeding?'

I felt proud as I told her I would be breastfeeding. I was no longer one of the formula-feeders; I was now part of a more elite group: the middle-class yummy mummies with their Bugaboos and designer changing-bags. (And yes, I realise how ridiculous that is.) She arranged to give me a call the following day to see how I was getting on and to arrange to come and visit us at home to offer any guidance or support I needed.

After waiting for the whole day, we were finally discharged at a quarter past ten that night. In hindsight, I wish we had pushed to stay overnight, as walking out into a cold October darkness was a huge shock to the system after pretty much being cooped up in one dark room for days. What's more, it was a shock that I didn't need.

I stared up at the rain-sodden sky as we walked back to the car and was suddenly terrified.

What the hell have we done?

CHAPTER 11

I'll Finish This if I Live Long Enough

I barely noticed the state of the house when we arrived home that night; that was something that could keep until tomorrow. All I could think about doing was collapsing into bed and trying to get a few hours of much-needed sleep in the bank.

Jacob was to sleep in his Moses basket next to me. I recalled the hours we'd spent choosing the right Moses basket: the whale-themed one with the rocking stand. And now I couldn't have cared less what it looked like; he could have been sleeping in a cardboard box for all I knew or cared.

It felt good to be back in my own bed, but also scary. *What if I have another bad night and lay awake until morning, feeding and settling Jacob?* I thought. *How will I feel tomorrow? Worse than I already do? That surely can't be possible!*

As it happened, this is exactly what did happen, so I had the chance to experience just how I would feel on another night of zero sleep. Jacob woke almost on the hour, every hour, for a feed. I began to feel scared each time he signalled he was hungry. It would start as butterflies when he began to stir, but my goal was always to get to him before the crying started. It was the crying I couldn't stand. It terrified me – I think it was an extension of my hallucinatory experiences, because I thought something dreadful and frightening was happening whenever I heard it. It just seemed like another sign that I was an awful mum.

To make matters worse, I couldn't get to sleep in between those horrible feeds. I was sore and uncomfortable and still heavily leaking fluids from the birth. On top of this, each feed would last for about 20 minutes at a time, meaning that, in reality, I only had 40 minutes in which to try to sleep before the next onslaught.

'I really don't think I can do this,' I wept to Michael.

Each feed was so painful that I cried through it and my body tensed up completely, which only served to make it even more difficult to achieve a proper latch, and, as Michael put it, that wasn't healthy for me or for Jacob. My husband was so lovely about it, which only made me cry more. Now that I was out of the hospital environment, I had lost the little confidence I had had with breastfeeding even with the little support I'd received there. I sobbed through each feed, my nipples dry, sore, cracked, and bleeding; I felt almost violated, as though my whole body was a wreck since giving birth. I felt that I might never feel okay again.

At some point during that night, Michael and I both made the decision that I would stop breastfeeding the next day and switch permanently to formula.

The next morning, Michael went out early to buy bottles, formula, and a steriliser. Although I still felt like such a failure for giving up on the breastfeeding so soon, I must admit that it was also a blessed relief. Now we could share the feeds between us and I would know that Jacob was actually getting the amount he needed. I wouldn't need to be frightened and in pain every time the time came for a feed, and I could claim back a little bit of my body for myself. Having said that, even the notice on the formula packet tried to guilt-trip me: "Breastfeeding is best for babies and provides many benefits." *Yeah, thanks for that. As if I didn't already know.*

As a new mum, I felt pulled in a thousand different directions. All the advice seemed conflicting and confusing. Swaddle, don't swaddle. Co-sleep, don't co-sleep. Breastfeed. Formula-feed. Mix-feed. It was endless and, on top of my wretched insomnia, wasn't helpful. It felt like we were just blindly making choices based on ... well, nothing tangible really. We just did what we could, when we could – anything that might make things that bit easier in the moment. And actually, if that's the way you survive and keep your baby safe, well, there's nothing wrong with that. Your instincts are there to be trusted.

Later that day, a lady from our local breastfeeding support group phoned to ask if I was still breastfeeding and to see whether the group could offer me any support. The sense of guilt hit me all over again as I heard Michael tell her we were now formula-feeding. It felt like I had let down yet another person with my selfish decision.

I was in a daze as I walked around the house that morning. It was funny; it seemed like my house, yet everything had changed. I just couldn't relate to it, or to any of my belongings lying around. When my lovely midwife, Jane, arrived to check me and Jacob over, she commented on how nervously I was acting – constantly jiggling my leg up and down, biting my nails and staring into space as I sat and spoke to her. This was to be the last time I saw her, before she handed me over to the health visitors and I was quietly panicking. Jane was the one who understood our story, the one who knew me. To the health visitors, I would just be another new mum, another patient number on a file. They wouldn't know how breakable I was, how much I needed looking after ... Through a cloud of unreality, I vaguely heard Jane telling Michael to keep an eye on me as I seemed quite detached. She had seen this in mums before, she said, and it could be an early indication of postnatal depression starting to kick in. She even made a note to this effect in my postnatal notes, which is why, in hindsight, I'm a little surprised that no other healthcare professionals picked up on it during later visits, despite my trying to articulate it to them several times.

I've a suspicion that nobody knew quite how to help me, so it was easier to sweep it under the carpet and hope I snapped out of it myself. Or maybe I should have tried much harder to articulate the way I was feeling. It's just hard when only the positives are being picked out and recorded in the red book; you start to feel rather as if you're imagining all the horribleness, or that maybe you've blown it out of all proportion somehow. Added to this was my knowledge that Amanda and Nicole were doing great with their babies, and the inherent need in me to be the same as all the strong parents around me made me hold back on making my true feelings known.

Jane said that mental health problems can be very common in women whose strict professional schedule is suddenly ripped away with the birth of a child. Everything they're used to is thrown into confusion. For example, I had still been expecting to sleep pretty much to the same pattern I always had, but that just wasn't possible anymore. Mums who are used to a more relaxed daily routine with no set times for eating or sleeping usually tend to fare better with this fluidity. If my experience has taught me anything, it's that I need a definite structure to my day in order to stay well. As he gets older, I can see that Jacob's exactly the same.

It was "unfortunate", Jane said, that Jacob was waking hourly for feeds, even during the night. 'It'll soon settle down in time, though,' she added cheerfully.

Well, I'd lost all concept of time, so that meant very little to me.

Mum and Dad came over after Jane had left and brought a big balloon with "Baby Boy" on it, along with some flowers. (Thankfully, I'd changed so many of Jacob's nappies by this time that I was pretty clear he was a boy, so the balloon didn't freak me out. If they had brought it to the hospital instead, it might have been a different story!)

It was though they were speaking in another language as they made small talk about what they had been up to. *So, there's still a life going on outside these four walls?* I wondered incredulously. My dad commented that a sheet that had been hanging up outside was dragging on the floor, and that we should go and sort it out before it got dirty. *In what universe is that even relevant?* I thought. I couldn't compute how he was actually saying these words. The sheet had probably been like that for days anyway, since before I went into hospital. It just wasn't important and I didn't have room in my head for it. It was as though reality had been suspended in my world; all I had space in my mind for was Jacob and sleep.

I had a major freak-out later that morning when I noticed Teddy eating something off the living-room floor. By nature, Devon Rex cats are very curious creatures, and ours has a habit of finding and eating any bits of debris from the floor, so we always have to keep our floors spotlessly clean. That day, the house was understandably far from clean, and there were bits of wrapping paper and other detritus all over the place from the presents and cards we had received. I managed to get Teddy's latest find off him before he swallowed it, commenting that the house wasn't safe for him at the moment. Mum, Dad, and Michael brushed it off and said he would be fine. However, the next time I went to the toilet I heard Teddy choking outside the door and knew he had succeeded in eating some scrap of wrapping paper he had found.

If it is this hard to look after a cat, how on earth am I going to keep a baby safe? I kept thinking.

I was screaming and crying as I tried to get him to throw it back up and it was only then that I was taken seriously with my concerns. Mum said that she and Dad would take Teddy home with them and keep him for a few days until the house was in better order. Much like with my mental health difficulties, sometimes you need to scream and shout before anyone hears you.

*

By now, I had had three hours' sleep in three days and was in quite a bad way. I don't cope without sleep at the best of times, and, coupled with the trauma of labour, I was going downhill rapidly. I felt nauseated and completely wired; my head was pounding and I was still having to change my pads several times an hour. And then there was the small matter of trying to keep up with the demands of a newborn.

'I'm taking you home with us,' Mum insisted. 'You need to get some sleep.'

I didn't have the strength or the inclination to argue.

Michael says now that he felt shocked that I was leaving Jacob so soon and that it seemed so far removed from my naturally maternal nature. He had imagined that the first few days would just be the three of us cuddled up together, but it was quickly becoming apparent to him that that wasn't going to be the case. He began to worry that there might be something wrong but, having never been through the experience of having a baby before, he also wondered whether it was just normal and so didn't say anything at the time.

Society has led us to believe that women should not be apart from their babies at all during those early days, and I am sure there are many, many women who couldn't bear to be, but I was not one of them.

I was ashamed at how good it felt to drive away from the house that day, leaving Michael to look after our tiny son. All that was on my mind was sleep, since I was sure I would be a better mum once I'd slept. I didn't miss Jacob at all.

The Small Faces' 'Itchycoo Park' was playing during that short drive. It's funny how, looking back now, I can relate my experiences to pieces of music that were playing at particular moments. Music was like some kind of connection to an outside world that was still going on in spite of everything, even though I struggled to find the enjoyment in it that I usually did.

Rolling into my old bed in my old room at Mum and Dad's, I felt a sense of excitement come over me. Sleep at last! But it did not come. In a tried and tested method, I started to read one of my old books, a favourite from when I was a teenager and nothing too taxing. As hoped, I started to feel a bit sleepy several chapters in, and was so thankful. But every time I began to drift off, I would jolt awake with butterflies fluttering deep in my tummy. I felt nervous and anxious, as though sleep was suddenly a frightening prospect. I think this was partly a natural instinct that had kicked in, that I wanted to be alert to Jacob's needs (even though he wasn't with me right then), but, unbeknown to me, it was also the start of a complex psychological battle I was about to embark on with my own brain. Sleep had become so central to my thoughts that I had become scared of it. It had become bigger than me. I was convinced I was going to die from the lack of it.

Eventually, I fell asleep. When I woke up, I leapt out of bed and ran downstairs, excited to tell Mum I had been to sleep at last. My joy was short-lived, however, when I looked at the clock and realised I'd slept for all of 10 minutes. Mum wanted me to go back upstairs and try again, but I knew it would only make me more anxious and thus more unlikely to be able to fall asleep. I also felt guilty for leaving Michael at home with Jacob for much longer, so she agreed to drive me back home.

Before leaving, I went back upstairs and bookmarked the page I had got to in the book I had been reading. Then I carefully pushed it right under the bed, so far under it that no one but me would ever know it was there.

'If I survive this,' I silently promised myself, 'if I live long enough, I'll come back and finish this book one day.'

*

That short car journey home felt like being driven to a funeral. The mood was sombre and the atmosphere heavy. I wasn't looking forward to being back with all those responsibilities and no opportunity to take care of myself.

When we reached home, my heart sank when I saw Michael's uncle's car outside the house. I remembered in that instant that Michael's auntie and uncle had arranged to bring my father-in-law over to see Jacob, but I still felt unjustifiably furious. I looked a mess – I *was* a mess. There was no way I could go in there and make polite conversation over a cup of tea! *How dare these people intrude on our home when we've barely been out of hospital for 12 hours?*

Panicking, wide-eyed, and hoarse from exhaustion, I broke down to my mum.

'I can't go in there, I can't! I at least need to go and get dressed before I see them – I'm still in my pyjamas!'

'Well, I'll take you back to my house then,' Mum said, trying to calm me.

'No, I can't leave Michael on his own any longer. But I can't go in looking like this!'

By now, I was almost shouting.

'You can, it'll be fine. I'll go in with you. When they see what a state you're in, they won't stay much longer anyway.'

I could tell that they had been discussing me over their tea while they passed Jacob around. It was obvious by the silence that descended over the room when I came in (I had clearly been able to hear them talking when I entered the house). Naturally, they found it strange that I would leave my three-day-old baby to go and get some sleep. Michael's auntie tried to tell me about how she had struggled with her sleep after being in hospital.

'It's the wrong environment,' she started. 'Noisy, too bright, machines buzzing all night. It took me a while after coming out to sleep properly again.'

I tried to nod along and be polite, but inside I was fuming that she would have the audacity to compare her situation with mine. She hadn't gone through the trauma of a long labour and birth. She had at least had some sleep, even if it was poor. I had become a horrible, bitter person in the space of a few days and that just made me hate my situation even more. This wasn't me; I was usually so happy and chatty.

They tried to chat with me for a while, but I behaved petulantly and lay down on the sofa, shutting my eyes and pretending to be asleep. I just wanted them all to leave – which they soon did.

Looking back, I am ashamed of my behaviour that day. Why shouldn't Michael have his family come and visit? After all, I'd had mine over. I ought to have been grateful that they cared so much but it was as much as I could do to wonder how they could be carrying on so normally when the whole world had changed for me. I hated them for being able to leave our house and go back to their normal lives, while I was stuck in this new and completely alien life of my own creation.

CHAPTER 12

Mismatched Socks

My friends have always played a pivotal role in my life. From first boyfriends, to university, to buying our first homes, they have been there for it all.

Jen, Amanda, and Heather visited the first night we were out of hospital. In their company, I felt relaxed for the first time in days. Amanda's youngest child, Harry, is only a month older than Jacob, and she brought him with her. He cried for most of the visit. I'd felt guilty and helpless whenever Jacob cried, but Amanda was so laid-back when it happened with Harry and simply laughed it off before giving him a feed or changing his nappy. It made me feel like perhaps I was doing an okay job with my son after all.

All my friends have breastfed their babies and I think the expectation (more from me rather than from them) was that I would do the same. They had always made it look so easy (I'm under no illusions that this wasn't actually the case) and so I had never really considered formula-feeding before giving birth. I felt nervous about breaking the news to them that I had tried and failed at breastfeeding, but I needn't have.

'It doesn't matter how he's fed,' Amanda reassured me. 'As long as he *is* getting fed, that's all that matters.'

A day or two later, my milk dried up. I wasn't prepared for the pain and sobbed all night as my breasts became engorged – the discomfort was immense! As well as the psychological impacts of ceasing breastfeeding, I was also now dealing with the physical ones. Michael was brilliant and literally held my hand all night as I cried.

Despite people's reassurances about formula-feeding, I continued to feel tense around Jacob. Whenever he was asleep, I would anxiously await him waking up, and whenever he was awake, I was willing him to go back to sleep. I felt like nothing I was doing for him was right and that I was messing him up. Each time he cried I would feel myself physically stiffen up with fear because I knew that signalled him needing something. *What if I can't give him what he needs and then he never stops crying and neither of us ever get any sleep ever again?* My thoughts all came out as one big muddle and I didn't know how to even start sorting through them all. Everything I did was geared towards getting Jacob to drift back off to sleep.

I dreaded Michael's two-week paternity leave coming to an end. When I took Jacob for his heel-prick test at a clinic a few miles away when he was a couple of days old, I tried to express this to the nurse who was carrying out the procedure.

'All new mums feel like that,' she said.

If she had probed deeper (or if I had had the courage to speak up), she might have been able to identify the issues that were starting to take root within me. Namely, that I was paralysed with fear every time Jacob cried, that I was worried I wasn't being a good mum to him and that I dreaded being alone with him. But because I found it hard to admit to myself, I shrank away from the issue and didn't push it when she said it was a common feeling that I was experiencing.

I also tried to hide my feelings from Michael. He is a worrier at the best of times, and I knew he was already concerned about me and worried about leaving me on his return to work. He told me he thought I needed to speak to someone, but I just kept brushing him off, not wanting anyone to know how miserably I was failing at being a mum after all the hoping and praying we had done.

He would try to give me advice that he thought might help. 'Forget about the clock. It doesn't matter when you get up or when you go to bed anymore. Don't try to live to your old routines, because you can't with a baby.'

Michael knows me better than anyone and could tell that something wasn't right, but my determination to appear strong and show that I was coping, coupled with the health professionals' assurances that my feelings were normal, meant that he accepted this as part and parcel of having a new baby.

If I could give one message to others who might be going through similar experiences, it would be to be as open as you possibly can about the way you're feeling. It'll be the hardest thing in the world to do, but it just might save your sanity, or your life, or both. Hiding your problems won't "disappear them", as Jacob says, but it could make you seriously ill, like it did for me. People can only help you if you let them in.

*

When Jacob was three weeks old to the day, I took him out on his first big trip. It was Nicole's oldest daughter's second birthday (she had given birth to her youngest daughter just six days before Jacob was born) and we had been invited to a local ice-cream farm with an adventure playground and sand and water play. I was wracked with nerves, and had been since the previous day. I had never been out for more than an hour or so with Jacob on my own before, and the practicalities overwhelmed me. *How will I warm his bottle when we are miles away from home? My friends won't be much help – they've all breastfed. How will I cope being out all day when I am so exhausted?* I was only getting about four hours of broken sleep a night. Would my friends even notice there was something wrong with me?

When I look back on photographs from that day, the one thing that hits me most is the outfit I had dressed Jacob in. He had on a grey Babygro with a robot design on the front, and the bottoms of the legs were tucked into bright red socks. It didn't match at all. To me, this is a clear indication of my state of mind at that time: I was confused and shell-shocked and completely overwhelmed at having to take care of this demanding little bundle by myself – I wouldn't have dreamt of putting him in such a mismatched outfit otherwise. But at the time, I either didn't notice or just didn't care.

As it happens, the day out went better than expected. I managed to get Jacob's bottle warmed up in the café with no issue. I even ate a bit of lunch myself, something I'd hardly been doing of late. I had time to talk to my friends and feel a little bit like the old me for the first time in ages. Jacob smiled his first proper, gummy smile. A brief but bright ray of happiness sparked up inside me when he smiled at me that day. *I must be making him happy at least some of the time, by some miracle*.

The only low point came when I was getting ready to leave and I had bundled Jacob up into his snowsuit for the journey home. Jen and Amanda were helping me load up the car and fasten Jacob in.

'You're not supposed to have them so wrapped up in the car,' Jen commented.

'I know,' Amanda agreed, nodding.

What have I done wrong now? I wondered. Is this something all mums just know? *Well, no one sent me the memo*.

Jen was, of course, quite right, but at the time I felt extremely fragile and vulnerable, and any comment to do with my parenting cut deep, even if it was said out of love. I pretended not to hear what they had said and just carried on packing the car and saying goodbye to everyone before driving away. I cried for most of the way home.

Over the next few weeks, I carried on as though on autopilot. I would go through the motions, responding positively when asked if I was enjoying motherhood and pretending to be enamoured with everything Jacob did.

'It's amazing the first time they laugh,' people would gush to me. 'Just you wait!'

While I was certainly pleased with those first smiles and giggles, they just seemed to prove that I was managing to hide my lack of feeling towards Jacob quite well. *Maybe he won't be too damaged by the way I'm feeling*. I was doing a good job of pretending and, for now, that was all I could hope for.

I tried to express my concerns on several occasions to the health visitors who came to see me. While they were great at talking me through the practicalities of Jacob's sleep patterns, feeds, and nappies etc., they did not seem to notice the way I was feeling. Of course, that's partly down to me, as I was still trying to hide it. I would only drop hints that were summarily dismissed as being normal and nothing to fret over. But I also think that they didn't quite know what to do with me, because my issues did not fit neatly into "classic" postnatal depression.

During the daytime, I would try to sleep when Jacob slept, but I just wasn't able to. The unpredictability of his naps, which might last for three hours or 10 minutes at a time, made it impossible for me to relax enough to sleep. I felt a fear in the pit of my stomach that I would suddenly be rudely awoken from my slumber by a crying baby wanting a feed, so I found it easier to not even try to go to sleep in the end. All it did was heighten the anxiety that I might be woken up.

From week three, I determinedly set out to try to firm up Jacob's bedtime routine. All the literature out there (and there's *a lot*, from books to blogs to forums) told me that this was the only way to ensure my baby would get into good sleeping habits and that it would pay dividends in the future. So, you see, even this act of seeming care and love was actually designed to make life easier for me. Mental health problems can make a person very selfish. They suck the empathy and compassion out of you and you can only think about yourself and how you feel. They are all-consuming.

My end goal was a full night of uninterrupted sleep, and I was damned if I wasn't going to do everything in my power to get it. So, from three weeks old, Jacob was bathed, fed, read to, and put down to sleep in a darkened room. During those early days, he was with us in the living room in his Moses basket, the lights off and the TV turned down so as not to disturb him.

It actually did work to an extent; from a few weeks old, Jacob was routinely sleeping from seven o'clock in the evening until eleven o'clock at night, waking for a feed and then going back off to sleep for another three or four hours. Ever since then (and even now) I have been militant about his bedtime routine, scared to relax it even slightly in case his sleep habits suddenly go out the window.

I regret now trying to be the same as how my friends were with their babies. It seemed like they were always gallivanting here and there, having big days out, and generally breezing through the whole babyhood thing. I wanted to save face, to show them I was coping as well as they were, so I tried to copy what they were doing. In the end, all it did was make me feel like even more of a failure when I came home exhausted and was too tired to look after myself or Jacob properly, and Michael would have to take over my duties.

I needn't have (and shouldn't have) tried to push myself so hard. It would have been much better to have taken things steadily and at my own pace, but at the time all I could think about was what everyone else would think of me if I stayed at home all the time or only went out very locally. I felt I was letting my friends down if I didn't keep up with everything they were doing, and I worried they would think I was letting Jacob down too by not giving him all the opportunities they were giving to their children.

When Jacob was about a week old, Becky had had an all-day crafting workshop for her hen party. Amanda went along with her baby and was genuinely surprised that I wouldn't consider going with Jacob.

'Why wouldn't you go?' she asked. 'You don't want to be stuck in the house all day when you could come with us.'

I wasn't quite sure how to say, without sounding silly, that I was worried about looking after Jacob on my own for a whole day and that I didn't want people watching me feeding him, winding him, settling him. I was still on a steep learning curve and I just didn't want to have to learn while people looked on. I wanted some privacy in those early days. So in the end I just made up an excuse; it was easier than telling the truth and having people think I was crazy.

I signed up for classes – baby massage, baby yoga, singing sessions, and swimming lessons –anything I could that would show how much energy I had and how brilliantly I was coping. I took Jacob into work, telling anyone who would listen how many activities we went to and how much I was enjoying every second of my maternity leave.

Eventually, I knew something would have to give. But for now, I was doing too good a job of hiding how I felt, and I wasn't going to stop anytime soon. I could not be a failure at the one thing I had pined for more than anything else: motherhood.

CHAPTER 13

Obsessions

As my mental health began to decline, so too did my sleep, even once Jacob's sleeping pattern became more predictable and he slept for longer chunks of time. One thing exacerbated the other: the less I slept, the worse I felt. The worse I felt, the less I slept.

Quite quickly, my old obsessive thought patterns began to reveal themselves again, like old enemies coming back to taunt me. This time there was a difference in that they affected me and my health to a chronic level.

I became all-consumed by thoughts of sleep: *When will I next sleep and for how long? What would happen if I never slept again? Is anyone else feeling the same way as me?*

I scoured the internet to find out how long it would take for me to die from lack of sleep. I found that my organs would slowly start to shut down and that there may be permanent damage done to the nerves in the brain and spinal cord, which may ultimately result in my death after weeks or months of not sleeping.

I would also obsessively research how many hours' sleep the average adult needs in order to stay well. Whichever article or study I had read on any given day would dictate how many hours

I aimed for that night. The first thing I would always do when I woke up in the morning would be to check my clock and then count back to see how many hours and minutes I had actually managed, and if I needed to deduct any time off for trips to the toilet that night. I would invariably fall short of my particular target for that day. This would then make me focus on how poorly I was feeling without the magic number of "sleep hours" I had convinced myself I needed, even if I hadn't been feeling poorly to begin with.

Once he realised I'd been ploughing through whole books during the night in fruitless attempts to get myself off to sleep, Michael convinced me to see the doctor about my sleep when Jacob was a few weeks old.

'I really think you need to go and speak to someone. I think you're becoming preoccupied with sleep,' he said gently. 'If you don't make yourself an appointment, I'll do it for you.'

'I'll do it.'

And I did. In a way it was a relief that Michael had said this to me – if he was taking me seriously then maybe the doctor would too.

The doctor prescribed Amitriptyline, a painkiller that can also be used to treat depression and help the patient to sleep. I started on 10mg a day and slowly increased up to 75mg. The medication helped to begin with, and I achieved my first eight-hour stretch of sleep on it at last while Michael took care of Jacob for the night. The day that followed that night was magical. We didn't do anything particularly monumental or exciting, but our trip to the park in the glorious fresh air and then to Mum and Dad's for lunch felt like a giant step forward. I was actually able to enjoy Jacob properly for the first time, and I got a glimpse of the mum that I was meant to be.

Having said this, the bad days still outweighed the good days significantly, and most of the time I felt like I was wading through treacle to get even the simplest of tasks done. It would usually take until lunchtime for me to get out of the house! For many weeks I was still having to use thick pads to control my post-birth discharge and I no longer recognised my own body. I could rarely find the time or energy to drag a brush through my hair, let alone to go out and buy clothes that fitted my post-birth body properly. I had always been a natural size eight up until my pregnancy, whereas now I was a 12–14. I had put on three and a half stone in total while pregnant, of which two and a half stayed on after the birth. With clothes shopping being the last thing on my mind, I tried to cram myself into my old clothes, often having to use elastic bands to fasten my jeans. I no longer recognised myself in the mirror; my face looked puffy and bloated, my skin was grey, and my eyes were framed with heavy black circles. I marvelled at how other women with babies seemed to have time to put on make-up or curl their hair when I couldn't imagine ever doing these things again.

The state of my body reflected the state of my mind and I didn't have the energy to change it. My obsessive thoughts ramped up a gear. It had got to the stage where I couldn't watch television, read a book, or even listen to music without searching obsessively for any references to sleep. Little by little, the things that gave me enjoyment in life were becoming a source of fear to me. Every time anything to do with sleep was mentioned – or even hinted at – I would hone in on it straightaway and become fixated. As a result, I stopped wanting to watch anything on TV for fear of what I might hear. The same was true for my beloved books. I was so frightened of reading anything to do with sleep that I just stopped reading altogether. Slowly but surely, I was losing my identity and starting to push the things I loved away. Very quickly, I began to feel like I was Jacob's mother, but not a person in my own right.

I was very strict with Jacob's routine, and made sure he went to bed at the same time every night. One evening, Heather invited us to go over to hers and she wanted me to bring Jacob as she hadn't seen him in a while. I agreed – under the condition that he would stay asleep in his car seat the whole time we were there and that no one would wake him up. Of course, when we got there, the girls all wanted to hold him and cuddle him, so my pre-conditions went out of the window. I felt sick with worry that he would be up all night after all the excitement, but needn't have worried. Jacob had his best night's sleep ever that night!

With my state of mind being as confused and clouded as it was, I lost all sense of what was normal and what wasn't. I knew that some of the things I was feeling were normal, everyday things that all new parents experience, and it was easy to convince myself that this was the same of my obsessive thought patterns (even though, deep down, I knew that it wasn't). For example, sleep is a hot topic of conversation amongst parents of babies, so I tricked myself into believing that my obsessions were just a part of that.

The only person I admitted anything to was Michael, and even then it was only a tiny portion of what I was feeling, as I was still trying to prove to myself that my feelings were nothing out of the ordinary.

One day, before the health visitor came round for her scheduled visit, the two of us talked at length about how I could try to explain my state of mind to her. I was awaiting her arrival nervously, terrified that any admission of my obsessive thoughts could lead to Jacob being taken away from me, just as the twins had been. I imagined that we must be on some kind of social services "watch list" – I had failed at being a mum to the boys, so now they were just watching and waiting for me to slip up so they could swoop in and take Jacob too. I wondered if I'd be better off keeping quiet just to save any hassle. But even that didn't seem such a horrific prospect at that time – a break from Jacob so I could try to get my sleeping patterns back to normal would be quite welcome; it was more the social stigma I was worried about.

When the health visitor arrived that morning, she had another lady with her. This new lady was doing the rounds with my health visitor on that particular day as she was training to become one herself. She also happened to be the wife of one of Michael's friends. We were asked whether it was okay for her to be present and I immediately said yes, not wanting to offend her. In hindsight, I should have declined; it just made talking about my problems that little bit more difficult. I felt awkward and as though I didn't want to admit to too much.

In the end, I tried to bring up the way I was feeling several times during the visit.

'Every day I feel as though I'm wading through treacle even to just get up and dressed,' I began, but was told this was common.

I explained how I hadn't even brushed my hair that day, but was told not to worry, that it didn't matter. But to me, it did matter. I wasn't myself at all. I broached the subject of not being able to sleep, but was told to paint the bedroom green, to try *feng shui* with the bedroom furniture, and to use a little lavender oil on my pillow at bedtime. They just didn't seem to be listening to me, and I was getting desperate. Inside, I was panicking that they were going to leave soon and still no one would know of my anguish, but I just couldn't seem to make them hear me. It was like I was crying out for help, but everyone was too polite to notice, or felt it easier to pretend not to. Like that bit in *Titanic* where Kate Winslet says, 'And all the while, I feel like I'm standing in the middle of a crowded room, screaming at the top of my lungs, and no one even looks up.'

In the end, I just nodded and smiled in agreement. If the health visitor had probed a little deeper during that visit, I'm quite sure I would have broken down and told her the whole truth, but at the end of our session, she ticked the boxes on her form and told me she would see me at the next visit. I felt so alone.

CHAPTER 14

Deeper into the Dark

Time passed by and I carried on caring for Jacob. I do not say I carried on "being a mum" to him yet, as I don't feel that would be a fair assessment of my relationship with him at that time, but I was at least meeting his needs. By comparison, Michael's relationship with Jacob was thriving; they had a lovely bond and Michael was always the one who could make our son laugh.

As Jacob got older and we started to wean him onto solid foods, I found that life with him continued to get harder rather than easier. If Michael noticed how much I was struggling, he never let on, perhaps out of some vague hope that one day everything would just be okay again. All he ever wants me to be is happy, so I think he felt so desperate for me to be my old self again that he was frightened to say anything in case it set me back further.

And anyway, on the surface, I was coping. Jacob was alive and well; I had managed that much, so what more could anyone ask of me? I sometimes felt like whole days had passed in which the only thing I had achieved was to clean up the Weetabix that had cemented itself to the walls. I looked forward to nap times so that I could just sit in silence and not have to be at the beck and call of my baby. On too many occasions to count, I fantasised about Jacob not being there at all. I wished no harm on him and would never have harmed him myself, but I found myself imagining if he had never been born and how all my problems would magically vanish if he simply was not there. I would also sometimes fantasise about what would happen if Jacob became ill and died. That way, I would be relieved of the social stigma of him being removed from me but would still be able to return to my former life and hopefully learn to sleep normally again.

I never seriously wished harm on my baby; they were just fleeting fantasies – but ones that I knew I must not tell anyone about. This makes me feel like an absolute monster to admit, but if I'm going to tell my story, I need to tell it all. I need to make sure that nothing is missed, because, just maybe, this book could be the lifeline to someone that I wish I'd had during the peak of my illness. I never want anyone to feel as alone as I felt.

Thinking about how I used to feel like that makes me so sad now. He was just a beautiful, innocent little boy born to a mum who was ill, through no fault of his own. He deserved better.

*

From 18 weeks old, Jacob had been sleeping reliably from seven o'clock in the evening right through until five o'clock in the morning. He had gone into his own room at three months old, despite the official recommendation being six months. It just made me anxious and on edge to have him sleeping in the same room as me; every grunt he made in his sleep had me wide awake and unable to settle again. Every decision I made was for a selfish reason, even though I tried to dress it up as being "best for Jacob". By now, I was so adept at hiding things that even Michael just thought I was acting as any good mum would.

However, my own sleep was still suffering badly, despite Jacob slumbering through the night. It was almost as though I had forgotten how to sleep. I could close my eyes and try to let my thoughts drift, but sleep was never the result as it had been in the past. I concentrated on getting my "sleep health" sorted out – no phones or TV for at least an hour before bed, then a warm, milky drink at bedtime in a clean bedroom free from clutter. Lavender oil on the pillow, and an interesting-but-not-too-exciting book to read to lull me into sleep. A completely dark room with no distractions. These were the well-rehearsed lines trotted out to me by anyone who came to know about my issues with sleep – health visitors, doctors, family, friends ... It was well-meaning advice, yes, but in my case, it only made me feel worse when none of them worked – I was too far past that stage at this point.

The Amitriptyline also seemed to have stopped working, although I carried on taking it in the hope it might suddenly start again.

My relationship with food also continued to worsen. Some days, I would exist on a glass of water and an apple. I felt as though I didn't deserve food, like I wasn't worth the effort of feeding myself properly. After all, I was a selfish mother who could only think about my own need for sleep – why should such a terrible person have the right to look after themselves properly?

I was also afraid of eating too much and vomiting; these were similar feelings to those of years before, when I was scared of eating in public. The difference this time around, however, was that I wasn't scared of people seeing me being sick; instead I feared not being able to look after Jacob properly if all I could do was to stay in the bathroom and hug the toilet. The only time I ate a proper meal was when it was cooked for me, and even then, I rarely managed to finish the food on my plate. Of course, this food deprivation only served to exacerbate my feelings of exhaustion. Everything I did required so much effort, and I felt as though I was 100 years old. I would literally have to crawl up the stairs on my hands and knees, and found carrying Jacob a real struggle. It was like I was looking in at my life from behind glass rather than actually living it.

Naturally, the way I was behaving caused tension in our family life. Michael wanted to go out and do things as a family on his days off, but I was often too tired to do anything other than sit staring off into space. Michael said that it was as though I was there but also not really there; the shell of my body was present, but my mind was somewhere far, far away.

'You need to start snapping out if it,' he said one day. 'I thought you'd be happy once we'd got a baby, but you're not. It's making life miserable.'

'I'm sorry,' I replied, still staring into nothingness. 'I'll try.'

But I couldn't even muster up the energy to do that.

Little by little, all sense of normality drained away from me. My existence was purely about looking after Jacob and trying not to die from lack of sleep. Occasionally I would still go out into the big wide world to meet with friends and family, but this became less often as time went on, mainly because having to keep up the pretence of being fine was so tiring. The "realness" of life and all the wonders it holds were out of reach to me at that time; my normal reality had been suspended indefinitely and I didn't know if I would ever get it back.

There were some things that could make me feel slightly better in everyday life. My parents were hugely supportive and I think they sensed something was wrong, although, like everyone else, they assumed it to be baby blues rather than anything more sinister. (Baby blues is a completely valid and proven condition that's likely to be caused by the hormonal change, and it's pretty common, so it's natural that that would be their assumption.) I would usually stay over at their house with Jacob a couple of times a week, when Michael was working a night shift. Just having someone else near to me in those dark, sleepless hours gave me comfort and hope that I might one day be okay again.

My friends, too, were supportive merely in the fact that they were close, both metaphorically and literally (they all lived about a 10-minute drive away from me). It meant that I could sometimes almost forget about the dead weights in my mind that were constantly dragging me down, and actually believe that better days were coming. It was a rare moment that I could really, properly belly-laugh in those days, but whenever I did, it was usually down to my girls. Sadly, these moments were fleeting and brief.

I was grateful that Jacob had so many people in his life that adored him and were willing to shower him with affection during those early months. It meant that, even when I was feeling at my lowest and felt I couldn't give him all the love he needed, he would always be able to get it from someone else. I loved Jacob insofar as I wanted to keep him safe and I wanted him to be happy, but that special mother–baby bond that's so often talked about was so far eluding me.

I was grateful, too, to know I had the support of those who love me. I know not everyone has that support network around them. I can only imagine what might have happened had it been just me and Jacob; there might not have been anyone there to catch me when I did eventually fall.

I have many photos of Jacob during his first six months that show him smiling and laughing, and they bring me great comfort that, in spite of the way I was feeling, I did manage to raise him as a happy little boy. I also have many fond memories of him that just make me roar with laughter now, such as the time he produced a poo volcano in the middle of the night that squirted several feet across the room (I wasn't laughing at the time, I can assure you!) and his confusion whenever Teddy walked into the room (you could almost see the cogs whirring in his brain – *is it a toy? What do I do with it?*).

I subconsciously longed for someone to break down the barriers I had so fastidiously put up and demand the truth from me. The pressure of keeping everything locked up inside was becoming too much. I had built walls around myself so that I could carry on being perceived as a "normal" mum because I hated the thought of being exposed to society as anything other than normal. I had to be okay; everyone else was okay and managing with their children. There was nobody in my family or circle of close friends that had suffered with mental health conditions, so I just didn't feel it was an option for me. I wasn't the kind of person that was supposed to be mentally unwell; it just wasn't the background I came from. What right did I have to feel like this? I, who had tried so hard to have a baby? I, who had had the twins removed in order to care for my biological child? I was sure I would be labelled as selfish and ungrateful. After all, my beautiful baby boy was here and he was healthy and I knew of countless others who hadn't been so lucky.

I wish I'd had the confidence to tell someone exactly how I was feeling. There were lots of times I had conversations in my head with faceless doctors; they were nobody in particular, but were a symbol of help and of hope.

'I don't feel well,' I would tell them. 'In my head. I'm struggling. I can't look after my own baby.'

'Don't worry,' they would reassure me. 'It's quite normal. We will help you.'

But, when it came down to it and when it mattered, I could never get the words out, so there they stayed, locked inside like a caged bird that's never been allowed to fly. I couldn't tell Michael as he was already worried about me and I thought it might send him over the edge if he knew my true thoughts. I wish someone had explained to me that postnatal mental illness doesn't have to fit neatly into a box, that it might not present itself as classic postnatal depression. That Googling "postnatal depression" won't give you all the answers you're looking for, because mental health problems are different for everyone. This is my wish for others, for the future.

CHAPTER 15

Do or Die

I have only ever had real, proper flu once in my life, and that was in April 2016, when Jacob was six months old. I had been feeling poorly for a day or two when, in the deep, dark hours of a Friday night, I woke bathed in sweat and unable to move. It felt like Satan himself was coming to claim me. Michael was working a night shift that day, so it was just me and Jacob in the house. I was confused and didn't really know where I was or how to work my phone, but I eventually managed to dial the only number I could remember: my parents' house. Apparently, I kept insisting to my dad that I was a robot, that my arms were made of a very heavy, cumbersome type of metal and I couldn't move them. We can look back on it now and laugh, but at the time it was quite a worry for them!

Luckily, Mum and Dad only lived a two-minute drive away at that time, so they hurried over and let themselves into the house. After trying and failing to move me off the bed – my limbs wouldn't seem to do what I asked them to and I could do nothing but lie there in the position they had found me in – they called for an ambulance. The paramedics quickly decided to transfer me to hospital because I was vomiting at an alarming rate and my temperature was dangerously high. Mum and Dad stayed at the house to look after Jacob and Michael met the ambulance at the hospital.

Although much of that night is a blur, I can clearly recall snapping at the poor paramedics to "shush" and telling them that there was a baby asleep in the house and that they mustn't wake him. Even in the height of my raging temperature and robot hallucinations, I was still obsessed with not disturbing his carefully planned routine – I just couldn't go back to night-waking after painstakingly getting him to sleep through! That I could even think about this in the midst of everything else just proves how fixed in my brain the topic of sleep had become. It was the centre of everything, the elephant in every room I entered.

Once I had been admitted, I was taken to Resuscitation as a matter of urgency, as my temperature was continuing to climb and it was suspected that I might have meningitis. I was still hallucinating badly – I could clearly see the *Scream* mask reflected in every shiny surface and instrument. I was given a lumbar puncture and several rounds of bloods were taken. Eventually, I was diagnosed with influenza B and transferred to the infectious diseases department, which was to be my home for the next week. The doctors also wanted to keep a check on my lungs, as I am susceptible to pneumonia and had already suffered with it twice before. Ironically, I had already had the flu jab that year, but it had been for a different strain!

Once the antiviral medication had started to work its way through my system, my temperature came down and the hallucinations subsided. Unfortunately, when my parents visited the next day, they told me that Jacob was also showing signs of illness and that the GP had referred him straight up to the hospital as it was likely he had caught the influenza from me. A few hours later, I heard that he had been formally diagnosed with the flu and admitted into the children's hospital, where he was receiving the same treatment I was.

I was worried about him. I didn't like the thought of him suffering and I blamed myself for ever having fantasised about him becoming ill.

Oh God, I thought, my heart sinking. *What if he actually dies from this and I wished it on him? What if he's frightened and in pain and he wants me, and I can't go to him?*

But I must admit that the overriding concern in my head that day was, *Man, this is really going to mess with his sleep pattern*.

Michael was incredible during that week. He split his time between visiting me and being with Jacob, even sleeping by Jacob's side for the entire duration of our stay. I was so thankful to have such a strong, caring man for both of our sakes. He was there for our son when I couldn't be, both physically and emotionally, and I will always, always be *indebted* to him for that. My sister, too, went above and beyond, acting as a mother to Jacob and making sure that everything being done was in his best interests, despite her having her own five children at home to care for. Sometimes it still hits me how amazing my whole family were to us at this time and I wonder what I've done to deserve such heroic people in my life.

I settled into my hospital room (for obvious reasons, everyone gets their own room on the infectious diseases ward) and started to enjoy my time away from Jacob. Once I knew that he wasn't in danger and just needed time to regain his strength, I relaxed and valued the time on my own. For the first time in ages, I could just sit and read a magazine uninterrupted, and I could once again enjoy reading or watching something on TV. Even just sitting on my bed watching *Casualty* one Saturday evening filled me with excitement – I could watch a whole programme without having to do a feed or a nappy change!

I am embarrassed about that now, but at the time, I didn't feel any shame about it whatsoever – only relief. In fact, the idea of having to go back to "real life" at some point filled me with a nagging feeling of dread.

Visitors were limited to Michael and my parents, and even they were restricted to short visits and had to wear face masks when coming to see me, so I was left blissfully alone for large parts of the day. I had a small team of regular nurses that were responsible for my care, and particularly enjoyed talking to Sue, a round, matronly-looking woman in her fifties. As I got to know her a little better, I knew that she was trustworthy and had her patients' best interests at heart.

It was once I had been relieved of the responsibility of caring for Jacob that I realised that my fears around not sleeping were rooted in my responsibilities as a parent. That is to say, if I had a poor night's sleep (or, indeed, no sleep at all), I might not be able to care for him properly. Now that I was only responsible for myself, however, thoughts of sleep did not hold the same fear for me as they usually did. Now, I could watch *Coronation Street* without having to be wary of hearing references to sleep, and I could read as many magazines as I liked! If I had a poor night's sleep, so what? I could always catch up the next day, at a time of my choosing. It was so freeing.

I was also scared, I realised, of becoming ill while in charge of Jacob. Lack of sleep has always made me quite poorly; if I consistently fail to get my eight hours, I tend to vomit and am unable to co-ordinate myself properly (struggling to put sentences together, aching joints that make even walking upstairs an ordeal, that kind of thing). It was this lack of co-ordination that terrified me – what if I fell while holding my son?

I feared that he would be removed from our care if I, the primary carer, was too ill to look after him properly. This scared me, not because of losing my son necessarily, but because I would surely be ostracised by my friends and family, and Michael would leave me. Then I would be left alone, which has always been a real fear of mine. I need to have regular company and people around me, otherwise I start to become very down and my self-care starts to wane.

Once again, I was thinking only of myself. Mental health problems can be very selfish like that. They suck the empathy and compassion out of you and you can only think about yourself and how you feel. It's all-consuming.

*

A few days into my hospital stay, reality kicked back in. I'd envisaged myself spending long, lazy mornings in bed when I got home, and feeling refreshed and ready to take on the world. What actually happened was that I realised my sleep was no better in here than it had been on the outside. It dawned on me that perhaps my problems were much more deep-seated and serious than I had thought, and not merely a temporary glitch that happens when you become a parent. After all, no one else seemed to have the thoughts I was having.

All week, the nursing staff, doctors, friends, and family had been expressing their sympathy at how much I must be missing Jacob; despite being in the same hospital, I wasn't allowed to see him due to infection fears. I would nod in agreement and say it was awful being without him, when really, I didn't feel that way at all. I was glad of the break. And it was at this stage that I realised that these feelings were far from normal; I just didn't know how to express them to anyone else.

Up until then, I had been taking my prescribed Amitriptyline as usual, but now I begged the doctors for something stronger. They gave me Zopiclone instead, on which I slept all night long! I felt so much better the next day. My vomiting lessened and I felt a little bit like the old me. And God, had I missed that feeling! I felt more positive about the future than I had done in a long time – I even started to look forward to going home and starting to create a bond with Jacob.

But, to my dismay, the Zopiclone had been a one-off and I was not prescribed it again the following day, despite all my begging and pleading. Zopiclone can be highly addictive and I suppose they wanted my mental state as a whole to be assessed before giving it to me again.

I didn't sleep a wink that night. It was as though every creak of a door, every flicker of a light, was amplified in my head and refused to allow me to drift off. My every sense was heightened and I remained wide awake until the sun came shining through the windows the next morning, its joyfulness at odds with my low mood.

'How did you sleep?' Sue asked as she came in with a hot drink for me.

'I didn't,' I replied.

She just groaned in sympathy and said something about people often finding it difficult to sleep in hospital. I can't blame her for this though; I wasn't telling the whole story.

I began to think about possibly telling someone in the hospital how I was feeling, but I was afraid of coming across as a drama queen. After all, I had already tried to tell my health visitor and been brushed aside, so why would it be any different now?

I fantasised about telling someone and being admitted into a mental health hospital, where I would have all my responsibilities taken away from me.

With any luck, I might be pumped so full of drugs that I would lose touch with reality, I thought. I wouldn't have to think anymore, or to make my own decisions; it would all be done for me. I might be deemed irreversibly insane and then I could stay here forever, sheltered, safe, and never having to do anything that scares me ever again.

Perhaps I might even get into a mother and baby unit, where I could have help with caring for Jacob but where the ultimate responsibility for him would be theirs and not mine. Being in such a unit would also negate my fear of the social stigma around having my son removed from me. And surely they would give me as much sleeping medication as I wanted if it made me feel better?

But who would I tell? One of the nursing staff? Sue? A doctor? Would they contact social services?

I worried that Michael would be angry with me if I did anything that might jeopardise our family unit. After all, my problems were my own fault; it was me that was obsessing over everything, me who was having these irrational thoughts. *Maybe*, I thought, *on some level I'm doing this on purpose, trying to shirk my responsibilities at home and with Jacob by making myself have these thoughts and stopping myself from sleeping. Maybe if I put my mind to it, I could just stop it all and be normal*. I worried that Michael felt the same way and would start to hate me for it.

The staff certainly seemed to have a lot more time for their patients on this ward compared to the maternity hospital, so maybe there could be a chance of having a proper conversation with someone. There was a lot for me to think about and only a little time left for action. I knew that the day was drawing near when I would be discharged, back to reality. Except I had a choice now: would it be back to my old reality, or could I make a change for the better?

CHAPTER 16

A Shifting of the Seasons

Word from the doctors quickly turned to my being discharged, and soon.

I knew it was now or never; if I left the hospital not having said anything to anyone about how I was feeling, the opportunity might not arise again. Here, in my private room, my thoughts were clearer than at home. I'd had the time and space to really think about what was happening inside my head, and I worried that, once home, it might not seem so clear-cut anymore. The daily grind of making up bottles, sterilising, feeding, mealtimes, and nappy changes, combined with a seemingly endless cycle of washing, housework, and trying to keep up with your own self-care, can tend to cloud one's innermost thoughts. It becomes habitual to push these thoughts down and not address them, demoting them to the bottom of a never-ending to-do list. It's easy for a new parent to see themselves as the lowest priority – their own needs become unimportant and "just something else to worry about", so it's easier to pretend they are not there at all. And that's completely natural, but eventually those needs will have to be addressed. If they're not, it can have serious and sometimes tragic consequences for the whole family.

As it turned out, I had a couple more days to pick my moment; it was discovered that my white blood cell count was almost non-existent, and so I would need to stay quarantined from the outside world until it had risen again, as any infection could prove disastrous for me.

The next day I woke with an awful feeling of dread, like a heavy stone had settled unceremoniously in the pit of my stomach. It was because I knew that day would probably be my last before being discharged. I could barely eat for the panic that rose up into my throat each time I thought of being left alone with Jacob again. By the evening, I had worked myself up into such a state that I was unable to leave the bathroom due to diarrhoea and vomiting. I sat on the floor next to the toilet, cradling my head in my hands, and I knew in that moment that this wasn't right.

I called for a nurse and asked for some anti-sickness medication. I was still in the bathroom when the nurse entered and I must have looked quite frightful, but he was clearly in a rush and just said he would get some brought down to me. In the end, the medication never did arrive.

Later that night, when the worst of the sickness had subsided, I lay tossing and turning in my bed, unable to sleep for the fear that was sending shivers all over my body. *Tomorrow*, I kept thinking, *tomorrow I'll have to start being a mum again*.

By about midnight, not having been to sleep yet, I called for a nurse. As luck or fate would have it, it was Sue who answered that call. I was already tearful when she came into the room and I begged her to try to get me some Zopiclone so that I could try to have a decent sleep before being sent into the big, scary world again.

It seemed an age, but eventually Sue came back with the single white pill that was the answer to all my prayers at that moment in time. *Why can't I take one every night for the rest of my life?* I wondered. *Who cares if they're highly addictive? At least I can function on them.*

By the time Sue returned with the Zopiclone, I was well and truly in the midst of a panic attack, although I didn't know it at the time. All I knew was that I couldn't breathe, couldn't stop crying, and felt as though the walls of my world had rushed right up to meet me, like a tide to a beach, crushing me and making it seem as though there was no way out. Sue didn't say anything at first; she just sat quietly beside me, hugging me close to her until I calmed down.

And then it happened.

Everything came spilling out in a big jumble, everything about not being able to sleep and being scared of my baby and being obsessed with the thought that I was going to die from insomnia. I told her how I wasn't eating properly and about my nausea and vomiting due to my anxiety. I told her that I didn't think I could look after Jacob and that I thought he would be taken away from me like the twins. The words toppled over each other like acrobats in a circus, and all Sue did was listen. She listened until no more words came, until a sense of relief at finally having got my emotions out washed over me. Until my panic attack reduced to just a few solitary sobs.

Eventually, when Sue sensed the time was right, she asked gently, 'Do you think you might have a bit of postnatal?'

The way she said it calmed me right down. It was as though, while she was acknowledging there was a problem, to her it was just another aspect of medicine. It was something that could be treated and that other people must suffer from. Not *minimalising* it, exactly, but normalising it.

I nodded in reply to her question as she told me her plan of action. 'I'll get onto your health visitor now, see if she can see you tomorrow when you're home.'

Although now very wary of the health visitors, I agreed because I thought they would have to take me seriously now, with another health professional referring me to them. Sue came back and told me she had left a message on the answer phone of my health visiting team, asking them to phone me the next day to arrange a visit.

As the rest of the night passed by and the next morning came up to meet it, I started to feel as calm and collected as I had done since before Jacob's birth.

Something was happening. The secret was out, and I could get the help I so desperately needed at last.

When Michael came to pick me up that lunchtime, I explained to him what had happened the night before. I was terrified he would go into panic mode as he sometimes does, and that I would then have to back-track and pretend everything was fine to stop him having a complete meltdown. This had happened, or nearly happened, a number of times since Jacob had been born. Michael needs lots of reassurance that everything is going to be fine, but with mental health issues this cannot always be guaranteed. So sometimes I would find myself trying to pacify him by saying things were fine when they actually weren't, just to keep him calm. That's hard to do when you're kind of crumbling inside. But I need not have worried. He listened patiently until I got to the end, then hugged me and asked how I felt about it all. I considered it for a moment.

'Okay, I think,' I ventured. 'I'm just relieved that it's all out in the open now and hopefully I can get some help.'

Michael can tend to have quite old-fashioned views and values, and believed prior to my diagnosis that we should each look after ourselves and that doctors and medical professionals are there to help with physical problems. We should deal with anything emotional or concerning our mental health ourselves; it's that old stereotype of the stiff upper lip. He could often be heard telling folk on the TV to "man up" and "take responsibility for yourself" whenever we watched something to do with mental health issues, and I was worried that day that he would have a similar reaction to my admitting to postnatal "depression" (you'll understand a little later on why I used inverted commas around the word depression). On the contrary; Michael couldn't have been more of a support to me. I believe that day that something clicked for him; he could finally see that there was a legitimate reason I hadn't been myself for all that time, and that getting the help I needed was key to me "coming back to myself" and to him. With Sue taking it seriously, he was able to accept that what I had was a medical condition rather than just an emotional state that would pass on its own. I would require proper treatment, and medication, and time and he was fine with that. He just wanted his wife back.

When he answered me, his words all came out in one big stream of relief. It was like he had been holding his breath, hoping that things would turn out okay, and now that I had acknowledged I needed help, he could breathe a little easier.

'I will support you, whatever you need.'

We spoke cautiously but optimistically during that car journey home. I think we both felt that relief – it was palpable – but we could not allow ourselves to get ahead of ourselves just yet. There was a long road ahead of us.

Jacob had already been discharged a day or two prior, and Michael had left him with my parents while he picked me up from the hospital. As we drove towards their house, I felt calm in a way I hadn't for over a year. I even felt a little pang of excitement at the thought of seeing Jacob after being separated for a week. Perhaps, with time and support, I could learn to be the mum I was meant to be, not just some imposter posing as a loving parent.

'I think I'm going to need time, and understanding, and lots of help,' I ventured. 'Do you think you can give that to me?'

'Yes, of course,' came his stoic reply. And I knew in that moment that he was serious. He would literally do anything for me, and I felt so fortunate. With Michael's quiet strength, I might just get through this.

CHAPTER 17

Facing the Fear

Sometimes with mental health problems, the physical symptoms can get somewhat forgotten. But let me tell you, they can be many and varied.

Before being officially diagnosed, my illness displayed itself in lots of different ways, so much so that I sometimes convinced myself I had some awful disease that would kill me even quicker than my insomnia would. When I say 'I suffered from extreme lethargy and felt exhausted', what I mean is that this was like no other tiredness I have ever experienced. My whole body felt heavy, like I was dragging a dead weight round all day. I'd be out of breath and light-headed even just walking upstairs, and would need to sit down. My skin became grey and very dry – I'm usually someone who wears make-up daily, but at that point I just couldn't bring myself to even look at my face in the mirror, so I stopped bothering. My face also appeared very bloated – when I look back on photos from that time, I can barely recognise myself. Add to that the aforementioned state of my ill-fitting clothes and I must have made for one hell of a sight! But I didn't have it in me to care.

No, that's wrong; I *did* care. I cared very much. I could see that Amanda and Nicole both looked great after having babies at the same time I did (and each with a two-year-old added into the mix!), but I simply didn't have the energy to change anything. I had checked out of myself.

So, on that first day out of hospital, I was determined that things would change.

The first thing I did was to go upstairs alone to see Jacob, who had been sleeping on Mum and Dad's bed. He was just starting to stir, so I lay next to him and stroked his cheek until he woke up properly. After a week apart, I expected he would be pleased to see me, would show me he had missed me. After all, I'd put up a good façade of being the doting mother, hadn't I?

Apparently not.

Jacob cried when he opened his eyes and saw me. He wouldn't let me comfort him, and only calmed when Michael came into the room. It was clear that his attachment to Michael far outweighed his attachment to me, and that hurt. It hurt deep down in my chest, a searing pain that spread to my stomach and made me feel a bit sick.

Instinctively, Michael understood that Jacob and I needed to be alone and he bowed out of the room without another word.

It had already been agreed that Jacob and I would stay with Mum and Dad for a few nights so that they could support me. I had been told I would need to rest for about two weeks as I fully recuperated from the flu, and I couldn't have done that without help (Michael was due to return to work the following day after having taken the week off to be with Jacob in the hospital). I was more than happy with this arrangement as I felt very weak both physically and mentally. My return to real life needed to be done gradually, both in a physical sense because of the flu, and mentally too.

Real life was a battle for me, and one that had no room in it for enjoyment. It had been a long time since I had been able to enjoy any of my own hobbies. It was like the old me had been lost for good. Instead, I must concentrate on Jacob's needs, which was a big mountain to climb in itself; I just didn't have the time or head space to think about doing anything just for me. I was in awe of anyone with a child who could do so!

My day would usually start at around six o'clock in the morning when Jacob woke up, and I would make up a bottle for him. After his milk, I'd try him with some solids – perhaps toast or Weetabix. I would then get him changed and ready for the day. By this time, I'd usually have already been up and about for a couple of hours (the clean-up after breakfast seemed to take an age) so I'd typically get myself ready for the day at about ten o'clock. I just did not understand how other people managed to be out of the house by nine (or even earlier)!

By the time we'd done an activity for an hour or two (a rhyme session at our local library, for example) it would be time to head home for lunch. I still wasn't really confident enough to take Jacob out to eat somewhere on my own, so I'd only do so with friends. I felt very self-conscious, as though people were watching me and judging my parenting; as though they might discover my secret – that I was only pretending to be a decent, loving mum. After lunch, Jacob would sleep for two or three hours and I would try to rest. More often than not, though, I would start to feel guilty 10 minutes in and get up to do housework.

When Jacob woke up, it would be time to start thinking about preparing the evening meal. Jacob and I usually ate together at about five o'clock, then I would keep Michael's warmed until he got home. Jacob's bath and bedtime routine started at six, so that he would be tucked up in bed by seven. Michael usually got home from work at half-past seven, then we would have an hour together after he'd eaten before going to bed ourselves.

The next day, it would all begin again.

I felt as though I was stuck in a hamster wheel, each day hardly differing from the previous one. I was scared of trying new things for fear of disrupting the routine Jacob and I had got used to, because I thought this might affect his sleep. It seemed my old obsessions of researching sleeping disorders and death from lack of sleep had been replaced by my new obsessive thoughts of maintaining *Jacob's* sleep now that he was more settled. I was starting to dissociate from myself and from life; I felt like everything was fake, like a movie set. Like I was in *The Truman Show*. At its worst, I would wring my hands so frantically that the skin would start to rub off and they would bleed.

The day I was discharged from hospital, my sister came over to Mum and Dad's to help me look after my son. Jacob picked up something sharp that was dangerous to him. Lizzie immediately called over to me to get it off him, but all I could do was look on vaguely, my eyes dull and unfocused. My brain slowly realised that I must stop Jacob from hurting himself, but I just couldn't get my body to react. And by the time I did, Lizzie had long since intervened. I think that was when she realised something was wrong. I vaguely registered her looking at me with concern, and all I could do was just wait for the health visitor to call.

Up until that point, I had only told Mum about the nurse's suggestion that I might have postnatal depression, but when I came down from the bathroom 10 minutes or so after that incident, Mum asked if she could tell Lizzie. I nodded in agreement. I really didn't care about anything anymore, least of all who knew about my problems. I wondered why this was happening to me, what I had done to deserve it. After all, Lizzie had three birth children of her own and had seemed to breeze through it all, just like my friends had done. I felt like an alien.

That afternoon, Mum and Lizzie must have been sufficiently worried about me to make me an emergency appointment with my GP. My memory is hazy, but at some point, Michael was called home from work, and he and Mum took me up to the surgery while Lizzie stayed with Jacob. I hadn't been out in the fresh air for decades, it seemed. Everything outside the car window seemed foreign and frightening to me. I couldn't comprehend how all these people were going about their usual business while here I was watching from behind a pane of glass, both literally and metaphorically. I had no connection with anything outside my little world anymore, and my grip on reality was slipping away.

When we got to the surgery, I panicked and tried to resist going inside. I was scared and confused, and didn't really know where I was or why I was there. It all felt very dream-like. I remember feeling like I was watching myself in a movie – I was hovering somewhere just above my own head and could see it all playing out as though I was out of my body.

They took me up to the second floor in the lift – I just couldn't have managed the stairs at all; I was far too weak. I was terrified of other people; every one of them was a potential tattler for social services, who might report me for being an unfit mother. Thankfully, the lovely, kind receptionist at the doctors arranged for us to sit in a side room.

After a time, the doctor came to collect us – the same one who had confirmed my pregnancy what seemed like light years ago. He was so kind, so gentle, that I was unafraid of going with him. I was so wired that I didn't feel as though I was actually there. I watched myself go into his office with Mum and Michael, sit down stiffly on the chair and start manically wringing my hands. The doctor put his hand out to try to stop me but I yanked them away, feeling like I needed to do it in order to be in control of at least one thing.

Michael was understandably upset and in tears, but I felt no emotional response at all. I merely looked over and acknowledged in my brain that it was happening. The doctor tried to reassure him, comfortingly patting his shoulder and telling him that his own wife had been through a similar experience with each of their five children. I just looked on, hearing what was being said but not really taking it in or relating it to myself. They could just as well have been talking about football results.

Following my consultation (which was mostly conducted via Mum and Michael answering the doctor's questions on my behalf) I was given a prescription for – *oh! Joy of joys!* – Zopiclone, and also one for Clomipramine, a tricyclic antidepressant that is most commonly used in the treatment of OCD, to take one 25mg dose per day.

The pharmacy we went to immediately following my appointment did not stock Clomipramine, as it is no longer commonly prescribed.

After learning of the desperateness of the situation, the head pharmacist walked to another nearby chemist to fetch some. It's little acts of kindness like this that I've experienced along the way that make me feel that someone, somewhere, is taking care of me. I've also come to realise that most people we encounter in life are lovely, caring souls and if it needed my illness to make me realise this, then I'm grateful for it. I still have problems getting hold of it to this day; the pharmacies local to me always have to order it in and it's regularly out of stock at the distributors, so I have to wait a while for it to come in. I've still never met anyone else who is on this particular drug, which sometimes makes me feel really alone all over again.

CHAPTER 18

2:00am is a Lonely Place to Be

My distress peaked that evening. My exhaustion was now so severe that I was running to the bathroom every 10 minutes or so to try to be sick. Eventually, my stomach must have been completely empty because I could only retch helplessly. I felt sick when I stood up; the only way I could get any kind of relief was to curl myself up into a ball and hold my tummy in a tight clench. Anxiety was washing over me in waves. *I can't take care of Jacob like this. What am I going to do?*

I huddled as close up to the wall as I could, trying to make myself into the smallest ball of a person possible. I flinched away when anyone tried to touch me, as that seemed to make my nausea worse. But then, everything made it worse, so I guess that didn't matter.

The panic attacks came thick and fast, and my mind was so clouded that I couldn't think properly. I couldn't tell Michael or my parents what was wrong – how was I supposed to tell them that it was *everything* that was wrong, that I didn't feel I could go on?

It wasn't that I wanted to die; I just wanted to sleep and then wake up and be someone different, someone normal. I fantasised about being totally free, maybe travelling in sunny climes, trotting from place to place without a backwards glance or a care in the world. Strange, really, as when I was younger and free to live that life, all I wanted to be was settled down and a mother. Funny how things come full circle sometimes.

The panic attacks all started to merge into one, like contractions in labour when the birth is imminent. I didn't want to talk to anyone, and I couldn't anyway. I wished everyone would just be quiet as each sound echoed tenfold in my head. I didn't want to be alone, but I didn't want to interact with anyone either. I needed to know they were there but couldn't converse with them. Their presence brought a certain comfort to me – I knew that, if I became really ill and started to vomit everywhere, at least people were there to look after Jacob. At that point I didn't care a jot about myself.

At some point, through the clouds that had settled all around me, I heard someone (it might have been Mum) phoning for an ambulance.

This was the last thing I wanted! I imagined myself being strapped to a stretcher and carted off to a horrible parody of a mental health institution, complete with padded walls and chains tethering me to the bed. I wouldn't be allowed to see Jacob again, which surely meant that our lack of a connection would only worsen until he eventually forgot I existed at all.

But there was also something deliciously appealing about the thought that maybe I could check out of life completely, that I wouldn't have to be responsible for myself or anyone else again. That I would be completely reliant on others to make my decisions, choose my clothes, and cook my meals. That I could sleep.

When the two paramedics arrived, it was apparent that they didn't know quite what to do with me, and I must make it clear that I don't blame them for this. They are not trained mental health workers, they are simply responding to a call from a switchboard. One of them asked why I was scared of them as I huddled closer into the wall and tried to stop them touching me. The truth is, it wasn't them I was scared of, it was the fear of making my nausea worse and vomiting all over the floor. If I was going to be sick, I wanted to do it alone, not with people crowding me and touching me. But I wasn't in a position to convey this at the time.

All the usual checks were carried out on me, including blood pressure and heart rate (which were, unsurprisingly, very high). The paramedics puzzled over what to do with me. They said that if they took me to A&E, I'd just be waiting round for hours to be seen amongst crowds of other people, which would only worsen my condition. They tried to find a place for me in our local psychiatric hospital, but there were no beds available.

One of the paramedics showed me some breathing techniques to try to bring me down from my panic attacks. These actually proved quite useful to me at a later stage of my recovery, but I was a little too far gone for them to have much of an effect that night. I kept on saying that I was going to be sick and that I needed to keep hold of the bowl I'd been clutching onto all night, but they tried to convince me I wasn't and took it away from me. Minutes later, I only just managed to grab it back in time before starting to throw up. As suspected, my stomach was indeed empty by then, so it was only evil-tasting bile that came up.

Eventually, after trying and failing to find appropriate help for me that night, the paramedics advised Michael to get back in touch with my GP the following day to see what other help I might be able to access.

Michael and Mum had to literally put me to bed. I felt dire and just couldn't stop crying and being sick. I took my Zopiclone and the Clomipramine, although I was aware that it would take a few weeks for the latter to start to have any effect. Mum stayed with me for a while until I calmed down a little and then she left me to try to sleep.

That night was the worst of my life. When I wasn't throwing up, I was tossing and turning, burning hot and almost hysterical through sleep deprivation. The Zopiclone had no effect that night because I was just too far gone, too wired, completely in the wrong state of mind for it to work.

By about two o'clock in the morning I had reached my limit. I went downstairs and lay on the kitchen floor, where it was nice and cool. Then I wished for death to come and get me. Come on, I'm ready for you now, I thought. For the first time, I seriously wished I could die so that I could get some blessed rest. *If I could only die, then I'd be asleep.*

I longed for it, but it did not come. It was at this moment I promised myself that, if I ever made it out of this alive, I'd turn my experience into a book and would make particular reference to the "2.00am witching hour". For me, two o'clock has always been the worst time, the time I am at my lowest. Two o'clock is the loneliest time in the world for a new parent who is struggling. It's such a solitary hour of the night; too late for even the night owls to be up but too early for anyone to be getting up yet. Once you hit about four o'clock, you can start to believe that morning is at least coming, that the world will start to wake up around you soon. But two o'clock is just bleak nothingness.

As I lay there, I could hear music coming from next door. It wasn't ridiculously loud or anything, but I could hear what sounded like 50's jazz seeping incongruously through the wall. I stayed very still and listened for a while. It was as though the music was telling me I wasn't quite as alone as I thought, and I took some comfort from that.

Eventually, I headed back up to bed. Mum must have heard me up and about, so she came in to see how I was doing. Her face fell noticeably when I told her I hadn't been to sleep yet that night. She stayed with me until it was time to get up and tend to Jacob, just stroking my feet and letting me know she was there, like she used to do when I was a little girl. It was a familiar gesture, a comforting one, and I longed to have the same kind of bond with Jacob one day.

But that day wouldn't be today.

That day, it was enough just to get out of bed.

CHAPTER 19

Losing Touch

That morning, Mum phoned the GP on my behalf and explained what had happened the previous night – what was still happening now. I couldn't bring myself to get dressed, so I sat downstairs in my pyjamas and refused to move from one particular chair, as I had convinced myself I would feel worse if I moved.

After a short time, the doctor phoned back, wanting to speak to me, so Mum and Michael left me alone so I could talk freely. The doctor asked lots of questions, and today, I felt more able to answer him. I just wanted someone to help me. I explained how I had become utterly obsessed with sleep, how it consumed my every waking moment and invaded my every thought. I confirmed that I had had obsessive thoughts quite regularly throughout my life, about the restrictive eating in my teens because of the notion that I might vomit if I over ate. The doctor re-affirmed that he had prescribed the Clomipramine because he suspected obsessive tendencies, and that the medication should, in time, help not only with the intrusive thoughts but also help me to sleep. He gave me the telephone number for my local mental health crisis team and urged me to call them; they would be better placed to help me on a day-to-day, practical level while I waited for the medication to take effect. In the meantime, I was to continue with the Zopiclone, which would be re-prescribed as and when I needed it. This was a huge relief; I had been worried about finishing the pack I had been given the day before and then being left in the lurch.

I called the crisis team as soon as I finished my conversation with the doctor. (I was worried that I would bottle out if I didn't do it straightaway). The lady I spoke to was so kind, so understanding, that I didn't mind going back through all the same things I had spoken about with my doctor. I knew I had to be honest in order for them to help me, so when she asked me whether or not I had considered suicide, I mentioned feeling like I wanted to die last night, but that I didn't think I would have seriously considered actually acting on it. She told me that this was a totally normal, common feeling that a lot of people get, which made me feel like less of a freak. The call concluded with her telling me that someone would be out to see me later that day.

It sounds trite now, but a measure of how unwell I was feeling at that time was that I didn't even consider getting dressed, washing, or brushing my hair before the visit. I just wanted to stay in my chair, not thinking, not doing, just being. I saw life carrying on around me, but I was frozen in time, stuck. I saw Michael taking care of Jacob, a job I should have been doing. I saw people come and go in the street outside. It was the rhythm of life, but my instrument was broken and I could not join in with the song.

Two ladies from the crisis team came to see me a couple of hours later. At first, I was left alone with them so that I could speak freely without judgement from Michael or my mum.

'They keep trying to tell me that Jacob's my baby, but I know he's not,' I whispered, desperate for someone to understand me.

'Why do you think he isn't your baby?'

'Because I can't look after him.'

To me, this made perfect sense. I wasn't able to take care of him because of how I was feeling, so therefore, he couldn't be mine.

I think I may have got a bit confused because of our connection to adoption – adopters are encouraged to tell their children that their parents loved them but weren't able to take care of them. So I thought Jacob couldn't possibly be mine anymore. Surely he was soon going to be adopted by people who could give him what I couldn't?

After a time, Mum and Michael came back into the room and I continued to talk to the ladies about how I was feeling. From what I've been told, I wasn't making very much sense, although everything seemed to add up perfectly at the time. I started to become paranoid that every car that passed the house, every person in the street, was coming to take Jacob away. Mum cried when she heard me say that I didn't believe Jacob was my baby, but I showed no emotion.

Why be sad? I thought. *He'll have a lovely life with someone who can take good care of him.*

My family were worried about my lack of interest in food and my apparent inability to stomach anything when I did eat. During those few days before, the only thing I could bear to eat and that didn't make me feel sick was fruit. I railed against being made to eat and it only made me more determined not to. The ladies from the crisis team had to gently encourage me to try to think about eating a small meal later that day.

Michael had been keeping my friends abreast of the situation on my behalf, as he knows me well enough to know that I would want them to know. We are in contact several times a day, so they would have been worried if I had just stopped contacting them abruptly. I realised just how lucky I am to have such close friends when I saw Nicole coming to the front door. She was coming to see if she could help in any way. It was so useful to have her with me for the session as she works in the mental health field – it meant that she was able to help me recap everything that had been said once the crisis team had left.

As the visit continued, I heard the ladies say to Mum that my condition sounded as though it was starting to tip over into postpartum psychosis. They said that I would need round-the-clock care and monitoring to make sure it did not get any worse. Mum assured them that I would be staying with her and Dad for the time being, and they arranged to visit again the next day.

Later that day, Michael took a call from social services. He was crying when he ended the call, so I asked him what had been said.

'They were just wanting reassurance that I have no concerns about Jacob's safety around you,' he told me honestly, 'and I told them absolutely not.'

He's lying, I thought to myself. *This is it. The beginning of the end. Social services will be round soon to take Jacob to a foster carer's house.*

Michael knew that the question was coming, but he says now that just hearing it actually asked out loud ripped his heart out. Even though he knew I was very ill, he never wavered in his belief that I would never, ever hurt Jacob. He says he felt so helpless that day, as though there was a glass wall between us. He could see me and he wanted to help me but he simply couldn't reach me.

That afternoon, I received a message from my friend, Jen, to ask if she could come round and see me that evening. I felt strangely nervous about it – not the thought of seeing her, but the possibility of still being up past ten o'clock (Jen is a notoriously poor time-keeper, so she probably wouldn't actually arrive until nine-ish). Ever since Jacob was born, I had rushed up to bed at the earliest possible opportunity in the belief that I would have more chance of falling asleep the longer I was in bed for. But I knew I had to push myself to see my friends, otherwise I would become isolated. And since I'm not a person who does well on long periods of being alone, I agreed to the visit.

Mum and Dad went out for a few hours that evening. I think they were just desperate to get out of the house, to have a conversation with someone other than me or Michael, and I totally understand that. Being with someone with mental health problems can be draining, and they were with me day and night at that point. They needed a break, as anyone would. Michael was also going to go out when Jen arrived, to meet his friend at a pub within walking distance from the house. I was nervous about being Jacob's sole carer for the first time in weeks, even though he was asleep by then and unlikely to wake up.

When I saw Jen pull up in the car, I started to panic. Amanda was with her, which I hadn't expected, and it really threw me. It wasn't that I didn't want Amanda there (these girls are like my sisters and always will be); it was more the fact that the plans had changed at the last minute and I didn't feel like I had any control over anything. Michael tried to reassure me and then went to meet the girls at the door, letting them know I was feeling anxious so they knew what to expect.

I don't remember a whole lot about that visit, but Jen and Amanda have filled me in since.

Says Jen:

I remember that day being really warm, and I'd gone to Derby with Amanda to get things for Heather's hen do. Then I saw a number flash up on the screen and my heart stopped – it was your mum's number and before I'd even answered I knew what she was going to say. I'd known for ages that things weren't right, but I didn't know how to confront it or what to say without making you feel worse. I will always feel guilty for that. You were struggling, but I just kept hoping things would improve over time. I've never said it to you before, but I am truly sorry for not trying to help you earlier, and I'll be forever remorseful of the fact that I could have helped you get the support you needed sooner.

Your mum was so worried and she had no idea what to do. Neither did I, to be honest, so I rang Nicole, who knew exactly who to ring and what to say to get you seen and on the right path. I told your mum that Amanda and I would visit you later that night, and we did. Nothing could have prepared us for how you were. You were unrecognisable, a shadow of your usual self. You seemed to go in and out of reality, able to converse with us one minute, and the next you were entranced, staring into space and rocking. Amanda's nursing instinct kicked in and she was amazing, holding your hand and telling you everything would be okay while I fought back tears. We were trying to make jokes about something on the TV, and at points you laughed with us, then at others it was like you weren't even in the room with us. It made me feel shocked and frightened; shocked at how things had deteriorated for you so quickly, and frightened that I wouldn't get my old friend back, my oldest friend who knew me so well and who completely got my bizarre sense of humour. But overall there was the guilt that we hadn't recognised how poorly you were and that, had we done something sooner, we could have helped you and prevented things getting to the stage they were at.

And Amanda:

You didn't really talk at all, and to be honest, I didn't know what to say. I'm not sure you'd have taken anything in anyway; you were in another place and no words would have mattered. We just sat for what seemed like hours in silence – I've no idea how long for. I just sat next to you and held your hand. I think you found some comfort in this. You were like a different person – not yourself at all. You were withdrawn, pale, and staring into the air – it was not nice to see, but that's what friends are for ...

Going to bed that night, on Mum and Dad's sofa while Michael lay next to me on an air bed (it was almost like being teenagers again!), I felt as though a weight had been lifted from me. In spite of how ill I had seemed to Jen and Amanda, I had indeed found comfort in their visit. It was as though, now that people knew what was happening, I could embrace the treatment being offered to me and not feel ashamed to accept help. I drifted off to sleep peacefully with a smile on my face, and I slept the whole night through (albeit with the help of a little Zopiclone).

But I was aware there might be hard times yet to come. It was one thing for close friends and family to know about my illness, but what about the rest of the world?

CHAPTER 20

A Delicate Balance

The home care team continued to visit me each day and I could be completely honest with them now – I *needed* to be, in order to start getting better. The team referred me to my local parent and baby unit, which is a service that supports parents during pregnancy and beyond, right through until the baby is 12 months old. The unit is specifically equipped to provide support to parents who are suffering from the perinatal psychological disorders associated with pregnancy and childbirth. The team felt I fitted the unit's criteria quite well, and an appointment was quickly made for me to attend it.

My first visit to the unit was at once both a terrifying and a healing experience for me. First of all, getting into the building itself was a big deal. There are two heavy doors to negotiate, opened by a combination of pressing bells, buttons, buzzers, and levers (or so it seemed at the time!) and I admit that I almost chickened out and ran for the hills while waiting to be let in. But I persevered, and was glad I did.

Once inside, I was shown to a cosy room where lots of parents were sitting around chatting. It was nice to see that a few dads accessed the service as well as mums. I was instantly made to feel welcome and I got chatting to a couple of other ladies – one turned out to be a former colleague of mine who was being discharged from the unit that day. Seeing how amazingly she seemed to be coping spurred me on to accept every bit of help that was offered to me.

I was assessed thoroughly that day so that the unit could decide what course of treatment would benefit me the most. My assessment was done through a combination of talking to a specialist mental health nurse and filling out the patient health questionnaires on anxiety and depression. I shocked myself with some of the answers I gave, such as the revelation that I had had thoughts of hurting myself or that I would be better off dead almost every day recently – I had no idea that things had got *quite* so bad for me!

They told me that they held a coffee morning there every single day of the week, so I could drop in if I felt I needed extra support. I can't even begin to tell you how much comfort this gave me. It was like having a security blanket to wrap myself up in whenever I needed it. I no longer had to do this on my own and I no longer had to wait for people to come over to the house. The support was there every day now; it was up to me to use it.

When I emerged from the unit later that day, I took the fresh air into my lungs and blinked up at the sun where it was peeking out through the clouds. I felt positive at a time when I'd forgotten what positive was.

A little later on, the staff member to whom I had spoken at the mental health unit phoned to let me know which services I would be offered. From my assessment, it was deemed appropriate for me to have weekly one-to-one counselling sessions, an indefinite number of appointments with a psychiatrist, and various group sessions that included breathing and relaxation techniques, Indian head massage, and play sessions to help me bond with Jacob.

I'm not going to pretend it was all plain sailing. There was one day when I felt so low that I dragged myself to the unit one morning and sat with my head down, not wanting to speak or look at anyone. I hadn't showered or brushed my hair, and I felt so disgusting. I just wanted to be taken away somewhere, to leave my life.

Through tears, I tried to tell the on-duty therapist how I felt.

'You tell me you feel like you've given up,' she began. 'Yet you sit here before me well-dressed, well-presented and clean.'

I didn't feel well-presented or clean – I still had yesterday's make-up on! And what did my clothes have to do with it? Was I expected to cut holes in them or roll in mud to make them look dirty each time I felt low? Clothes are just clothes. I felt like my feelings were somehow being dismissed because I didn't look "ill" enough. I was a little bit taken aback considering her professional status, but I suppose mental health professionals need some way to gauge mental wellbeing, and this may be just one marker that's taken into consideration. Either way, it was a blow. That was a bad day for me; a day where I felt like I was back to square one.

On the whole, however, my time at the unit was an overwhelmingly positive experience for me.

We discussed the physical symptoms of my illness as well as the psychological ones. I think the physical aspects of mental illness can often get overlooked. Before my own illness, it would never have even occurred to me that mental health issues could manifest themselves physically, but let me tell you, they can and do. I would ache from head to toe as a result of crippling exhaustion, and I found even small tasks overwhelming. Even walking from A to B could leave me overcome with tiredness and needing to sit down.

Then there were the compulsions that were a physical manifestation of my OCD. I would continually bite and pull at the skin around my nails until they bled, and I would pick at the skin around my nose until that bled too. I would also feel compelled to pull at large chunks of my hair to get some kind of physical relief from what was going on in my brain. These were my coping mechanisms.

I was now on 100mg of Clomipramine as I still found it difficult to sleep on any less, even when combined with the Zopiclone. My meetings with the psychiatrist helped to confirm that I was on the right medication at the correct dosage. The psychiatrist and the home care team were all very impressed that my own GP had had the knowledge and foresight to prescribe Clomipramine as opposed to other more common medications, and this helped to continue to build my faith in him. My doctor was on it; he knew the score. He was the bee's knees.

The relaxation and breathing sessions, as well as the Indian head massage, were conducted in a private room away from the babies. The babies were very well looked-after by specialist nursery nurses, with a strict ratio of staff to babies while the sessions were taking place. I was thoroughly assured that Jacob would be okay, that he would be brought to me if he got upset, that I could leave the session and return to him at any time. Understandably, lots of parents who attend the unit are very anxious about leaving their child, and there can be lots of tears from both parties. I, on the other hand, was at the other end of the spectrum and was probably happier than I should have been to leave Jacob; I was *excited* to have that time away from him. He never once had to be brought to me and was always playing happily when I returned to the nursery.

As the weeks and months passed by, I noticed that he would get more and more excited each time I returned, and he started to crawl over to me with a smile on his face when he saw me. It was proof of the bond that was finally starting to strengthen between us. I also started to get excited to see him myself, and I actually looked forward to it, rather than lamenting the end of each breathing session. When this began to dawn on me, it instantly made me feel happier and more content with life – although it did surprise me because I'd never before imagined I would feel anything like that. I hadn't dared let myself imagine it.

The sessions themselves were enormously helpful. I learnt how to relax enough that I would be in the right state of mind to fall asleep. One of the most useful things I learnt was that people suffering from anxiety often clench their jaw without even realising it and this tension can be one of the main factors in preventing sleep from occurring. Even now, if I'm finding it difficult to drift off, I'll check to see if I've unknowingly clenched my jaw. I often have!

I learnt how to breathe properly and not in the stilted, shallow way that people with anxiety often do. Sometimes that was difficult, especially when my nausea was at its highest because this deep breathing tended to make it feel worse. I was still terrified of being sick, especially when I was supposed to be taking care of Jacob.

I learnt about honing my sizeable imagination to create scenarios in my head that would help me to relax before sleep. One night, I could be walking down a beach and listening to the sound of the sea and the gulls circling overhead. The next I might be sitting next to a magnificent fountain with the water droplets descending all around me and landing softly in the basin. The scenes would invariably involve water of some kind; I've always been drawn to water, whether it be the sea, a river, or simply the rain. Michael often jokes that we always end up next to water whenever we have a day out. I find it so calming, so relaxing. On the recommendation of the unit, I bought some relaxation CDs made by a local lady and listened to them as I was getting ready to fall asleep. None of these things solved my sleep problems on their own, but they all helped.

My sleep itself was still both precarious and precious, as though it were the point of a diamond balancing delicately on the point of another diamond, and a small puff of air could send it all toppling once more. Some weeks, I would have five nights of decent sleep followed by a couple of rubbish nights, but this still felt like heaven to me. On the advice of my counsellor, I stopped counting how many hours and minutes I had managed and instead started to focus on whether I felt well and okay to take the day on or not.

Gradually, the home care team withdrew and I was left in the sole care of the parent and baby unit. I also had the support of my amazing GP, who had specified to the reception staff that I must be seen that day if I phoned up needing an appointment. Around this time, I was given my official diagnoses of OCD (which manifested itself in the obsessive thoughts about sleep in my case), anxiety, and severe insomnia, a combination of perinatal mental health conditions that had been brought about by a mixture of the hormonal changes in pregnancy and the trauma of the failed adoption. I had always thought of myself as being mentally strong, so it took a while for me to get my head around the fact that I now had this illness. It would never really go away; the best I could hope for was to manage it.

'You had always been, emotionally, the stronger out of the two of us,' Michael says now. 'So it was a shock, but also a relief, that there was something that explained the way you had been acting. It gave us something to work together on, as a couple.'

The rest of my family and friends were just as understanding outwardly – mostly. I sensed some degree of scepticism from one or two people that the way I had been acting had an actual name, was something palpable and that there were reasons for it. I don't think these thoughts were spiteful or malicious at all; I just think some people found it more comfortable to believe that I was "just a bit down", as everyone gets from time to time, and that I would recover quickly and be my old self again.

I still felt very fragile, almost childlike, and still very frightened. But I was making progress, and that was all anyone could have hoped for.

CHAPTER 21

Going Back

On the day of my first counselling session, I was shaking with nerves. With medication, you just take it; with the breathing techniques and the visualisation, you are taught what to do and then go away and practise them in your own time, in your own space. The thought of counselling, however, made me feel vulnerable, exposed. I would have to confront my problems head on rather than just masking their symptoms. I would have to face what I had been hiding from.

The therapist had a lovely, calming presence about her, which put me at ease straightaway. She was professional, yes, but also approachable, so I found I didn't mind chatting to her. I also found that, since she was removed from my situation, I didn't mind unloading all my negative thoughts onto her. I find it harder with friends and family, because they so badly want me to be okay, so I sometimes I tell them what they want to hear rather than the truth.

'I want you to go right back to when you first noticed a change in your mental health,' she began.

I could pinpoint almost the exact moment I started to feel ill. We had our matching panel around about the same day, so I could actually answer with complete confidence on this one – it was when I fell pregnant but before I found out, just before we started our adoption introductions with the twins.

We explored the ways in which my pregnancy had masked the joy I should have been feeling at gaining two beautiful sons, even though I didn't know it at the time. It became apparent that it was my body and my developing hormones making sure that I put the baby growing inside me first. These hormones can, amongst other things, make a woman feel as though she has lost all control of her emotions, which is what I believe was happening to me during those early days with the twins. I felt – and was – physically sick whenever they cried during the night, and I felt desperate and extremely anxious, as though I didn't know where to put myself or what to do with myself. I used to pace aimlessly all over the house – and quickly, too; I just couldn't keep still because the anxiety was so heightened. I was genuinely scared. I felt trapped and unable to get away from the situation. I wanted to bolt from my newfound responsibilities but I couldn't. Even now, I can feel that old fear start to rise whenever I recall those days.

During the next few sessions, I began to understand more and more about how I had been feeling. I learnt that my shame and guilt was largely unfounded and certainly not helpful to the boys, myself, Michael, Jacob, or anyone else.

'It's helping me to see that we did the only possible thing we could have done when we disrupted the adoption placement,' I told a friend at work one day.

She paused for a moment, thinking, recalling. 'You know,' she began, 'I was once told by somebody, when I was feeling ashamed about a situation that I felt I had caused, that "it happened because of you, but it wasn't your fault". I think that's something you need to hold onto.'

That phrase made complete sense to me and helped me to view everything in a clearer light. It has stuck with me ever since.

My therapist helped me to realise that so many huge and traumatic events had happened in my life in such a short space of time that it would have had a negative effect on anyone's mental health. There was the marriage, the infertility, the adoption, the pregnancy, the adoption disruption, Jacob's birth ... boom, boom, boom, one thing straight after the other, no breaks, no breathing space. And there still wasn't any breathing space now, because caring for a young baby doesn't allow that.

I also saw that I'd been holding a lot of my emotions in so as not to panic Michael, when I should have just been open with him. Having the counsellor confirm this to me spurred me to go home and discuss everything. It gave me a free pass to unload my feelings to my husband because I'd been advised to, and he wasn't allowed to panic! (I made him promise that before I began.)

'I feel such shame about the boys,' I told him, the barriers coming down at last. 'My heart breaks a little bit every time I think about it. I wonder where they are, what they're doing, who they're with. I wonder if they're okay.'

'I feel exactly the same,' he said softly, kissing my forehead.

We talked and talked about it, like we never had before. We opened up to each other and explained how we both felt about what happened. And then we hardly ever spoke about it again. We needed to have that talk so that we could clarify our reasons for doing what we did, and agree that we did the right thing and that the decision was out of our hands. To find, not peace as such, but at least a way out of the turmoil. But to this day it remains too painful to keep on going over it. I hope that one day we'll be able to talk about it again, to find some peace, but for now it still hurts too much.

For now, we content ourselves with hanging their carefully wrapped gingerbread men on the Christmas tree each year and quietly reflecting in our own way, occasionally reminding each other of a memory we have about one or other of the boys or a hope for their future. Come New Year, we pack them away again in their delicate white tissue paper. One day soon, I'll write them a letter each, tied up with ribbons that are the same colour as the gingerbread men; one blue, one red. I'll tell them everything and the reasons and I'll pray for their forgiveness and hope that one day they might come and find us so that I can hold them close again and tell them again in person. But that day's not now; it's not today. Some wounds take longer to heal.

Above all, my therapist and I spoke about Jacob and my feelings towards him.

'I worry,' I said to her, 'that one day he'll ask me what I felt like when he was born, and I'll have to say I felt nothing.'

'Do you ever ask your parents that question?'

I realised she had a point. She told me just how common it is for mothers not to feel that immediate connection to their babies, but the competitiveness of our society makes us panic if it doesn't happen straightaway. Once I knew this, I was able to let go of my guilt somewhat and start to concentrate on building that bond from then onwards.

'I'm also terrified that he'll develop mental health problems because of me.'

'He's no more likely to than anyone else,' she reassured me, very matter-of-factly. 'Your problems have been as a result of perinatal mental illness, which is not hereditary. Also, you'll be more aware than the average parent out there, so you'll be looking out for signs anyway and so will likely spot any problems early on.'

That the therapist dealt in facts was very reassuring. I like things tangible and scientific when it comes to my health, so I found her assurances to be of great comfort to me. Everything I told her, no matter how terrible it sounded in my head, was explainable. As soon as I said the thing out loud, it would lose some of the fear it had held for me. For instance, it is apparently very common for new parents to feel they want to run away, or for their baby to not be there. This knowledge was power to me. I no longer felt so alone and could start to move on, rather than get hung up on every single thought or feeling that came my way.

Counselling on its own was not a magic solution to all my problems, though. Nor was medication. Nor were any of the techniques I learnt at the parent and baby unit. But together, they all gave me a fighting chance of coming out the other side.

CHAPTER 22

Turning Point

Right up until the day of Heather's hen weekend, I still wasn't sure whether I could face going or not. *Will I feel strong enough to be away from home, away from Michael, for two whole nights? What if I don't sleep and fall to pieces?*

Michael thought it would be good for me to concentrate on something other than my illness for a while, so he gently encouraged me to go. My counsellor agreed and we spoke at length about how I could prepare myself for the time away.

'You're going to need to make sure you've got the support you need. Make sure the friends you trust and who know about your issues are there. If you can share a room with some of them, that would be really helpful. So that if you're struggling with your sleep and have a panic about it, they'll understand,' she told me. 'And take your Diazepam with you, and your Zopiclone. Even if you don't need to take them, they'll be there as a safety net for you.'

'What about drinking?' I ventured. I felt silly for asking this – as if it mattered in the grand scheme of things! But I do enjoy a social drink and knew I would fancy one when I saw everyone else having one.

'Well, drinking on your medication isn't advisable,' she replied. 'But we do understand that there's a real world out there. So, a small buck's fizz, sipped over a few hours, would be fine. But if you feel any ill-effects, stop straightaway.'

And so, tentatively, I set off that afternoon to the cottage that had been booked for the festivities. I had decided to travel in my own car rather than go with the rest of the girls so that I always had the option to come home if things got too much. Besides, it was only about an hour away so it wouldn't be a big deal if I did need to leave.

Pulling up outside the cottage, I felt my stomach start to flip when I saw all the other cars parked there. I knew there would be lots of people there who I didn't know, who didn't know me and my situation. I took a few deep breaths and went inside. Immediately as I entered the cottage, I felt panic rising and I just stood there and let it. Everything I had learnt about staying calm flew from my head, like birds that have been disturbed deserting an abandoned building. I needed to see my friends, but I couldn't see anyone I knew.

I took in the number of people who were there and started to feel sick. *How will I ever be able to sleep with all these strangers here? What if they want to stay up all night and my fragile sleep pattern is knocked off course again?*

I bolted for the door.

Outside, I raced to the car and jumped inside as quickly as I could. Once I'd locked the doors, I felt like I was in a safe place again and could begin to bring my panic levels down. Recalling the breathing techniques I'd learnt, I started to stabilise myself, to find my centre.

It took a long while before calm started to wash over me. I couldn't even say how long it took. I was preparing to drive away when Amanda appeared at my window. Gratefully, I unlocked the door. Without putting pressure on me, without any expectations,

Amanda talked to me and started to understand how I was feeling, then gently asked if I would like to have another go at going inside with her.

I've come this far, I thought, following her inside.

Once I was with the girls, I felt safe again. *Maybe I can do this after all*. Nursing my buck's fizz for the whole evening while everyone else was merrily quaffing the wine, I felt a bit out of sync with them at first, but gradually I started to relax and even enjoy myself. By the evening, I was having such a good time that I almost forgot about sleep altogether – this was something that was unheard of at that time!

The entertainment for the evening was provided by a murder mystery company who specialised in risqué, double-entendre-type scripts. I knew it was going to be a good night when the lead actor of the company phoned up while they were en route, asking whether we had a hot tub at the cottage to use as part of the performance!

'Are you sure he didn't say hot dog?' I asked Jen, when she came off the phone. 'Maybe they haven't eaten yet?'

'It was definitely hot tub.'

We dissolved into laughter.

By the time the weekend came to a close, my stomach hurt from laughing and I felt properly like me for the most sustained period of time since giving birth. And something else miraculous happened too – I really and truly missed Jacob for the first time and looked forward to getting home to him. It was such a clear, tangible moment, and one that still sticks out to me now. It was during the second day and we were sitting outside in the glorious sunshine, just chatting and listening to music. A couple of Heather's friends who I hadn't met before were asking what I did for a living.

'At the moment, I'm a mum,' I replied. And I felt so proud in that moment I couldn't stop smiling for the rest of the day.

The realisation hit me like a ton of bricks: I was proud of Jacob and proud of myself. He was alive, I was alive. He was happy, I was getting there.

So this is what it feels like to be a proper mum, I thought to myself – and it felt great.

I also had a breakthrough with my sleep that weekend. I used high doses of sleeping medication for the two nights we were there. Even so, I didn't manage to fall asleep until the early hours on the second night, but despite this, I didn't completely fall apart the next morning. I was tired, yes, but I felt like I could cope with it for the first time ever!

I was rather irritated, however, at hearing Nicole snoring and Amy sound asleep within minutes of getting into bed ...

That's so unfair! I thought to myself. But the difference was that this time I felt equally as amused as I did panicked. *The buggers!*

That felt significant. I'd not been able to find humour in anything for a long time, but that weekend started to change that.

*

From that weekend on, my mental health slowly started to improve. The weekend had given me a little bit of *me* back, and that's so important for recovery. After all, I only know how to be me, so starting to lose myself felt like being cast adrift. I didn't know myself, didn't recognise the person I'd become.

Together, my doctor and I managed to find the right balance of medication for me (100mg per day of Clomipramine, Zopiclone and Diazepam as and when needed). After monitoring my Zopiclone use thus far and noting that I was using it only as and when I most needed it, (rather than taking it as a matter of course), my doctor consented to re-prescribe it to me on this basis, for as long as necessary. Although the side effects were (and continue to be) unpleasant and include severe constipation, frightening and vivid dreams, an extremely dry mouth and memory loss, I was willing to cope with them rather than the alternative.

As soon as I started to feel consistently better (and by this, I mean when I started to have more good days than bad), my relationship with Jacob transformed. I found I could now show him affection and really mean it, rather than just doing it because it was what I thought I should be doing. I started to love him quite fiercely, which took me by surprise. It's a protective kind of love, in which I know to my core that I will look after him and shelter him from anything bad ever happening to him. I found myself wanting to spend time with him, rather than feeling obligated to do so. I began to appreciate the things he did and wanted everyone else to know how amazing he was. At long last, I was Jacob's mum.

With this bond becoming stronger every day, and with me feeling like me again at last, the rest of my life started to fall back into place as well. My relationship with Michael began to strengthen once again; I think he felt he was getting his wife back rather than being my carer. I started wanting to see people again and go out and do things. I looked forward to nights out and being with my friends. I started to do things for myself again, to enjoy things that had previously felt flat and flavourless.

One weekend, the girls and I went out for cocktails. I was so excited in the days leading up to it! I knew that I could be 100% myself with my friends, not having to watch what I said or did, and that I would never be judged. I bought a new dress – it was flowery and blue and short, perfect for hiding my mummy-tummy while still allowing me to feel okay about myself (my legs had survived pregnancy and birth relatively intact!). Michael told me to take as long as I wanted to get ready, so I had a long soak in the bath with a glass of wine, then spent a couple of hours on my hair and make-up. I felt pretty good once I was ready, and it shows on the photos from that night – I'm almost glowing with happiness.

Tentatively I had started to enjoy food again, so there were also some lovely meals out with Michael – our "thing" as a couple has always been to go out to fancy restaurants once every few months. It felt as though we'd taken a forced hiatus from our ordinary lives, but that it was now starting to get back on track.

Of course, learning to live with a long-term mental illness takes time. You are the same person as before but a slightly different version: you have to adapt certain things and consider whether you can still do everything you want to do at the drop of a hat, or whether particular situations might need a bit more thought and forward-planning. For example, if I'm staying away overnight somewhere, I have to make sure that the environment is going to be conducive to sleep, and would need to take my earplugs and sleeping medication. I also try to make sure that I won't be sharing a bed with anyone (other than Michael, who I'm used to!), as this can make me quite anxious and stop me from creating a calm mood before bedtime.

I started to be honest with people about the situation and was amazed at what happened. I have genuinely lost count of the number of people who have volunteered information about their own mental health issues when I have been open about mine. When you're in the thick of it, it can feel like you are the only person in the world who has ever gone through anything like this, but that's just not the case. People who I always thought seemed so "together" have told me things about themselves that I could never have dreamt of – people who I never imagined would tell me these things. It's as though, once the floodgates open, they can't allow them or don't want them to close again.

So, come May 2016, things were on the up for me. But that's not to say it's all been plain sailing since then. There was more to come.

CHAPTER 23

Diving In

In the months that followed, my relationship with Jacob went from strength to strength. At the parent and baby unit, I would be overjoyed whenever Jacob came looking for me when I went to make a drink in the kitchen, wanting to know I was still there. I felt like he had confidence in me as a mum now, and that boosted my own confidence in turn.

As summer turned into autumn, Jacob mastered walking, completely of his own accord, in two days flat. I say walking, but actually he skipped that part and went from crawling straight to running, and he hasn't stopped since.

I was encouraged to sign up for a "relationship play class", which taught how to strengthen the parental bond through all the different kinds of play. Every new class I signed up for (and I did them all – baby massage, baby yoga, swimming – you name it!) was another little win for me and Jacob as a twosome. Our relationship was at last becoming cemented.

This was evident during one swimming lesson in particular, when Jacob was especially tired. He hadn't slept very well the night before, and was happy enough being in the lovely warm water but wasn't up for doing much swimming. All he wanted to do was to cling on to me. The feel of those chubby little hands around my neck and his head on my shoulder was one of the most delicious feelings I'd ever felt. He needed me, I needed him, and together we were going to be an unbreakable unit forever.

I also started to feel less anxious about taking him for days out. I had previously worried that tiredness might overcome me if I ventured too far from home, but this began to lessen and the voice inside me telling me to stay in, just in case, quietened down.

When my 12-month maternity leave came to an end, I made the decision to hand in my notice and concentrate on Jacob and my own wellbeing for as long as necessary. Michael and I had been discussing this for a while, going back-and-forth and weighing up the pros and cons. Eventually it came to the crunch time when I had to let my work know either way.

'Look, you've missed out on a lot of the fun side of your maternity leave through being ill,' Michael said. 'And you're still recovering. I don't think you'll ever regret having more time at home with Jacob, but you might regret going back to work too soon.'

I could see that he was right, and fortunately our small house and our savings would enable me to do this for a year or so. I felt happy and comfortable with this decision and actually looked forward to spending this time as a stay-at-home mum.

As Jacob's first birthday came closer, I started to feel nervous at being discharged from the unit. I knew I was only eligible to attend until he turned one and then I would either be discharged or referred on to other services. Some weeks, I was relying on the support of the unit and the knowledge that I could go there at any time to get me through. My counsellor and I spoke at length about this, and it was eventually decided that I would be strong and capable enough to be discharged completely, which I admit I freaked out about at first. However, I knew now that I had the tools with which to help myself: the breathing techniques, the visualisation methods, the ways of rationalising my feelings rather than being terrified of them. I also had the contact details of all my support networks (including the crisis team, whom I could call upon at any time if I found myself in crisis) and I had my medication. All of this support acted as a safety blanket for me, because I knew that the help was still there if I should need it, even if I never had to actually call upon it.

Then one day, as my leaving date was drawing near, I got asked by one of the staff at the unit if I'd like to come along to a coffee morning run by our local branch of the national foundation PANDAS (Pre and Postnatal Depression Advice and Support). The organisation is a service that individuals and families can access for support – no need for a referral – and they offer a range of help options to suit individual circumstances and needs. I'd not heard of PANDAS before, but with the promise of tea and cake, I was there!

When the day arrived, I was feeling nervous as I got ready for the session but hung on to the fact that it was to be "informal". For people like me, in the grip of anxiety and other mental health issues, informal is great. Informal means you can leave at any time; informal means you can participate or stay on the fringes; informal is non-threatening.

Once I was settled with my Battenberg, a PANDAS representative popped over for a chat. We talked about ordinary things – last night's *Corrie*, how Jacob was doing with his crawling and what I enjoyed about coming to the parent and baby unit. It felt so natural to just be chatting mum-to-mum that I told her how I was soon to be discharged from the unit due to my son's age, and how I was feeling a little cast adrift by this.

'Why not come over to one of our groups then? We just have a laugh and a cuppa and if you want to talk about your illness that's fine, but if not, that's fine too.'

Before I went home that day, I was surprised with a lovely self-care pack that had been put together by PANDAS. In it there was a gorgeous scented tealight, a bath fizz, some sweets, and a little positive affirmation on a card that I put up on the fridge when I got home. When my mental health problems were at their worst, I felt as though I didn't deserve to look after myself or to have nice things, so being given this small gift was a way of telling me that I was worth something and that someone was thinking of me. It made me feel a little less alone.

Sure enough, once my time at the unit came to an end, I started attending my local group and never looked back. PANDAS truly caught me when I was about to fall off the radar of my local NHS services. And, as I tell other parents, your mental health problems don't magically fix themselves once your baby turns one, so don't be afraid to take advantage of any support that is offered.

By the time Jacob's birthday arrived, I felt well enough to celebrate with all our family and friends. Rather than a formal party, Michael and I decided to hold an open house, so that people could come and go as they liked and there would be more of a relaxed feel to the day. I wanted Jacob to be surrounded by those who love him, and I made a point of taking lots of photos so that he would never doubt how many people care about him. At that point in my recovery, that seemed like the most important thing in the world. I wanted him to be able to look back and know that, even when I was at my lowest points and could only offer him the most basic care – and, sometimes, no care at all – there was always this huge pool of amazing family and friends helping to raise him. It takes a village to bring up a child? In our case, it was more like a town.

But it would be wrong of me to say that my issues hadn't left a deeper impact on me. The guilt I had felt at being unable to breastfeed still haunted me most days and I used to sit and cry about the fact that I had "failed" where everyone I knew seemed to have succeeded. This guilt was compounded by all the pro-breastfeeding messages in the media and on the parenting sites I visited. Even if it wasn't true, I felt like formula-feeding was demonised at every turn and I wondered what long-term impacts it could have on my son.

'Formula-fed babies get ill much more. This could be anything from infections, eczema and other skin complaints, to sudden infant death syndrome, diabetes and leukaemia.'

'They are more likely to be obese.'

'You won't bond like you would with breastfeeding.'

It was relentless.

During the summer of 2016, I began to look into the possibility of "relactation", whereby a mother can return to breastfeeding even after a long break, or perhaps never even having breastfed before. I did lots and lots of research with the larger breastfeeding organisations and found that there was a lot of support to be had, but ultimately I knew it would be down to me, my tenacity and desire to do it, and my body's willingness. I tentatively contacted a specialist in the field and told her my concerns and my overwhelming desire to return to breastfeeding. She was very encouraging and told me about some techniques I could try, including breast compression, the right diet, nipple stimulation, and lots of skin-to-skin contact. She also recommended some supplements that could help. I was excited – surely if I followed her advice to the letter, my plan couldn't fail?

When I told Michael what I was planning, he was understandably concerned.

'I just don't want you putting any more pressure on yourself,' he told me. 'Jacob's doing fine; he's a big, healthy boy and you haven't done any damage to him by not breastfeeding. You had to do what was right at the time.'

For a few days, I tried to produce milk. The first time I actually put Jacob to the breast, it felt so natural, so right, and he seemed to instinctively know what to do this time around. But it soon became apparent that no milk was coming, and he started to get frustrated. I would sit there in tears, willing my body to do what I wanted it to, just this once. But it let me down again, I felt, and, after a few attempts I conceded defeat and gave up again, this time for good. I felt all the old emotions flood through me again: disappointment, failure, and an overwhelming sadness. Never again would I be able to breastfeed my son. To this day it still amazes me that mothers have breastfed for millions of years. It should be the most natural process in the world, yet it can be so, so tough. Why has Mother Nature made it that way?

Despite this, my mental health remained on a fairly even keel as 2016 came to a close and 2017 breezed in, and I felt okay – even good – most days. Any anxiety I had harboured about not being a good mum started to melt away as I saw what a happy and healthy little boy Jacob was growing into. This was brought home to me the day I watched Jacob study the twinkling blue lights on our Christmas tree. He stared at them, transfixed, for a good few minutes, then slowly raised his hand, pointed at the tree, and said, 'There.'

A huge smile spread across his face as he looked from me to the tree, wanting to show it to me. He was turning into such an eager little learner, wanting to know about everything and interact with everyone. He was fine, he was normal, he was surviving.

Coincidentally or not, as this began to happen I also started to feel a yearning for something else, which completely took me by surprise. Up until this point, I hadn't really given work a second thought, other than as a means to stay in touch with my friends there. Six months had passed by since I'd given in my notice and I was enjoying my time with Jacob. But I found that I started to feel envious of working mums; they seemed to have the best of both worlds – a great relationship with their children because their time together was "quality time" that they made the most of, and they had the benefit of extra money coming in and the independence of doing something for themselves. They had their autonomy back. They were having their cake and indeed eating it. That was the way I saw it.

At first, these were just thoughts, and not ones I mentioned to anyone else. But, slowly, I began to start looking around at the kinds of jobs that were available, feeling a spark of excitement about the possibility of "getting back out there". I knew I wanted to work in education again; I had experienced my six happiest working years in my employment with the school, but at that stage I wasn't sure exactly what type of role I would go for. Yes, there was excitement, but it also scared the hell out of me, and I didn't dare actually take the next step and apply for anything. For now, just looking was enough.

CHAPTER 24

Progressions and Regressions

I'm not sure if I believe in fate, but I do believe that things in life usually end up working out for the best, even if it takes a long while and a twisty path to get there.

One of these twists happened in February 2017, when my old job unexpectedly became available again. As soon as I found out, I phoned Michael at work to ask whether he thought I should apply. He was obviously wary of upsetting the delicate state of my mental health now that I was starting to feel better, but could sense the excitement in my voice as I talked about the possibility of going back to work.

'How would it work?' he asked. 'Would Jacob have to go into full-time childcare?'

'Well, you get Fridays off and Mum and Dad have already said they'd be happy to have him a day a week if I do go back to work, so it'd just be three days in nursery.'

Michael worked out exactly how much I'd need to be earning to make it worthwhile for me to go back, once the nursery fees had been taken into account. I was overjoyed to see that the salary would make it viable.

'If it's what you want,' he went on, 'then I think you should go for it. I actually think it'd be really good for your mental health to be back in a routine.'

Going into school for the interview felt natural and was like coming home. My nervousness soon subsided on seeing my old friends and students. Hardly anyone knew in advance that I was coming in for the interview, so to see such genuinely warm reactions from everyone was lovely. And the moment I learnt that my interview had been successful was magical; it felt as though my life was becoming three-dimensional again. It was further proof that I was getting my old self back.

During the following two weeks, I prepared myself for my return to work, part of which was to find suitable childcare for Jacob. My role is a full-time one but is term-time only, so I would have the best of both worlds – doing a job I love while still getting lots of spare time to spend with my son. We decided to look for a nursery for three days a week; my parents would take care of Jacob for one of the other days and Michael for the second one, as fortunately his job allows this. It felt important to me that he should be with family for more days than he was at nursery. As it happened, the nursery within walking distance of our house was rated outstanding by Ofsted and we had heard excellent things about it, so we arranged to go for a look round.

We loved the atmosphere of the nursery straightaway and it was clear to see that the children there were loved and nurtured by the staff. The room Jacob would be going into was light and bright, with a small ratio of children to staff, which meant that they were all getting lots of attention and input. There was a small line of prams in the little garden area outside and the babies were all wrapped up and peacefully sleeping in the fresh air, which was lovely to see, as I'm a big believer in the benefits of nature and natural light and air for children. There were toys and books and photographs on the walls of all the activities the staff did with the children. But what I noticed most of all was the air of calm and contentment that radiated from each child; I could see that they were genuinely happy there and it was clear that the staff adored them all. A date was set up for the following week for Jacob to spend some time there without me, which would be followed by a half-day before he started properly the week after, when I was due to return to work.

The first time I left Jacob at the nursery on his own was a strange affair. It was the first time we had been apart since I had really started to feel better many months before. He cried when I handed him over; I managed to keep it together until I got outside and into the car, where I had a little cry myself. The following two hours seemed like forever and I missed him so much, I was counting the minutes down until I could go and collect him. My mum and dad's house is only a two-minute drive from the nursery, so I went there to have a cup of tea and a bit of company to distract me, but I was still clock-watching!

As it turned out, Jacob had stopped crying as soon as I had left. He'd had a great time and settled really well with the other children. This made the second session a little easier for me to cope with and helped me see that it didn't make me a terrible mum to put him into nursery, something that we as mums are made to feel sometimes. I have heard comments in the past such as, 'People shouldn't be having children just to put them into nursery; what's the point?' But I also think the reverse is true – stay-at-home parents are also criticised for not working and allowing their child to socialise and learn in a nursery setting, and for not setting a good example of being a productive member of society. As mums – *as parents* – we just can't win.

Settling back into work the next week was hard in some ways and glorious in others. Now I could speak to other adults whenever I wanted, could make a hot drink at any time, and could eat my lunch at a sensible hour. But I also missed Jacob right through to my core. My love for him was now complete and all-consuming, and I just yearned to be with him all day long.

It was a primal, thirsty feeling, and I cried every single day that first week – I just wanted to be with him, to hold him, and take in his smell. Now, I could actually relate to the other parents at work who were telling me their experiences of putting their children into childcare for the first time. I was no longer just nodding along, pretending I understood what they meant; I was amongst them, and recognised the feelings of sadness they were talking about. That could only bring me some relief and comfort. I also appreciated these anecdotes because they showed me that Jacob would be absolutely fine and would settle in in no time at all.

As the days went on, however, and I slotted back into work mode, the benefits of employment soon became apparent. With my mind now being exercised daily, combined with a strict routine of six o'clock wake-ups and ten o'clock bedtimes, my sleep improved yet again. I hardly ever needed to take the Zopiclone anymore and it felt amazing! I was no longer waking up with the hungover, disorientated feeling that the Zopiclone creates and which often lasts until lunchtime, and my mouth no longer felt like sawdust or had the vile Zopiclone taste. Instead, I could taste freedom, and it felt good!

Could I soon be free of my Clomipramine too? I wondered.

One Friday evening after I had gone back to work, I realised that I had somehow let myself run out of Clomipramine. I can see now how it happened; my forgetfulness meant that I'd been meaning to get my prescription for days now but only seemed to remember this at night when I went to take my tablets, rather than in the daytime when I could have actually done something about it. In a state of anxiety, I told Michael what I had done. It took him a long time to calm me down and persuade me to call somebody for advice. After being referred to the NHS's 111 service, I spoke to somebody who said I would be able to obtain an emergency prescription from my pharmacy. However, when I phoned my local pharmacy, the pharmacist on duty got very angry, saying that he wasn't allowed to give emergency prescriptions for mental health-related drugs.

He was shouting down the phone, 'Why have you been told to call here?' as though I would know the answer.

By now a quivering wreck, I burst into tears and just kept saying I was sorry. At this point, Michael took over the call from me and the issue did eventually get resolved so that I got my prescription. However, the experience really took its toll and made me feel somewhat distrustful towards the health service once more. My confidence was once again in tatters – why was I being dismissed and belittled while Michael was being listened to and respected? I was grateful that I had him there on my side, but what I really wanted was my independence back. I'm a strong, intelligent woman, but I was being treated like a silly child. It got me wondering what would have happened to me if I had been alone, like so many people are, and didn't have the support of someone close to me. I certainly wouldn't have been able to begin the journey to recovery without having so many people around me, advocating for me, taking on the phone calls, being forthright and insistent when I was too weak to be. Maybe I wouldn't even be here at all without them.

*

That summer, Michael and I were fortunate enough to have our offer accepted on our dream home: a four-bed detached house in the neighbouring town that most of my friends lived in. We felt it was time to move on and make a fresh start at last, and we had long since outgrown our tiny chocolate-box starter home. With me now working again, we could at last afford to move.

Before moving, I made one last appointment with my GP, the man who had seen our whole lives change and had been there through it all. As well as wanting to thank him for all he had done for us before we moved to our new practice, I also felt as though I might be able to reduce my dosage of Clomipramine and wanted to ask his opinion.

'I don't see any harm in that,' he said, much to my relief.

I was to switch from 100mg per day to 75mg initially, with the caveat that I go back up to 100mg if it didn't feel right. I was excited to see whether I could exist with the reduction. If I could, maybe there was hope that I might not spend the rest of my life on medication.

I felt the difference of the change almost immediately. My head was clearer and I was less "zonked" as Michael put it. Since being on the medication, he had struggled with my memory loss and how long it would take me to process even the simplest things he said to me. Now, he told me, I seemed more alert and less "away with the fairies".

I began to have bigger and better ideas off the back of this success. *What if I could cut down again? I might be even better on just 50mg!*

Foolishly, I didn't see a doctor to discuss this second reduction. I thought I knew what I was doing, having given myself false confidence with the first, and so I reduced my dosage just a couple of months later.

Following this, my sleep began to deteriorate again, so I started to use my Zopiclone tablets more frequently in the hope that it was just a passing phase. I also started to have spells of dizziness more frequently (one of the side effects of Clomipramine is dizziness, but this can worsen during withdrawal). I also noticed that I was becoming more irritable and anxious than usual, but I tried to dismiss it as just being a result of stress at work.

I see now that these were warning signs and that I should have gone back up to the 75mg, but at the time I was so desperate to come off the medication and just be "normal" again that I ignored them.

I was also having some trouble obtaining my prescription from my new surgery. At my old surgery, my prescriptions would be sent electronically to the pharmacy so that I could pick up my medication without having to physically hand over the paper copy. My new surgery insisted that they needed to see a paper copy of an old prescription before they could re-prescribe the medicine for me, which of course I did not have. I started to feel so stressed about this that I felt I needed to try to ration the tablets I had left, in case I could not get another prescription. And so it seemed like the perfect time to reduce my dosage again. My sleep became erratic again and I started to obsess over it once more. I naïvely told myself that this was just a setback, that it could have happened even if I was still on the 100mg.

I limped along like this for a few weeks more before cutting down again to 25mg. My body hadn't had the chance to process all these different changes; I was changing things far too quickly and without medical advice. As far as my doctor knew, I was still taking 75mg. After this latest reduction, I began to feel really quite unwell, but I managed to hide it. (The first few months of my illness had taught me how to hide things effectively, how to explain things away, how to brush things under the carpet.) My sleep quality nosedived and I began to have dark thoughts again – thoughts of dying from a lack of sleep or being sectioned and taken away from my family and friends.

My thoughts became so skewed that I was struggling to distinguish real life from my illness, but by now I was the master of deception and an expert at hiding it, even from those closest to me. I convinced myself that I could do away with the medication altogether now; I could get better on my own by using my relaxation and breathing techniques. Looking back now, I realise it was my OCD coming into play here – I was becoming so obsessed with ceasing my medication that I was happy to lie to myself and pretend I didn't need it. I had had enough of taking medication, full stop.

Within a day of two of being off the Clomipramine altogether, my mental health crashed to rock bottom once more. With my mind in a haze, I had managed to mix up the dates of Jacob's check with the health visitor and only realised as I was getting him ready to go. Something made me check the appointment later and I saw straightaway that I was a day early.

I went from 0–100 in two seconds flat. I was in full-on panic mode. I had booked the morning off work for nothing, and might not now be able to get the next morning off too. *Would nursery even accept Jacob two hours late so that I could get to work for at least part of the morning?* My head was swimming, I couldn't think straight, I was hot, I was panicking, and Jacob would just not *keep the hell still* while I got him dressed –

I screamed. A proper, from-the-pit-of-my-stomach scream. A horror movie scream.

And, worse than that, I aimed it at Jacob.

I will never, ever, forget the frightened look on his little face as I, the person who was supposed to love and protect him, screamed at him. His face just crumpled as he burst into tears. Blindly, through tears and sheer panic, I managed to dial Mum's number and just kept sobbing at her, 'I can't do this, I can't do this.'

I couldn't process anything she said to me, but I do remember hearing her say, 'You're scaring me,' before telling me to stay where I was and she would come over.

Putting the phone down, I grabbed Jacob and held him as close as I could possibly get him to me, rocking him and saying into his hair, 'I'm sorry, I'm so sorry. I love you so much,' over and over again.

I must have sat there for 20 minutes or so before Mum let herself in and came to find me.

'It'll be alright,' she soothed, stroking my hair. 'It'll all be alright, you'll see.'

CHAPTER 25

Evolution

Mum and Dad were amazing, and took over straightaway so that I could once again start the process of picking up all those little pieces of myself that had shattered and putting them back together. Mum phoned work to let them know I'd be off for a little while and got me an emergency appointment with a doctor for that morning, while Michael came home to support me and look after Jacob.

Throughout that morning, I kept having the urge to hurt myself by yanking chunks of hair out. I found I could lessen this feeling a little by gripping chunks of my hair, close to the roots, really hard without any hair actually being pulled out. It was like a frustrated feeling, frustrated at the way I was feeling and thinking that I needed to punish myself by hurting myself in some way. This has happened on occasion since that day and I just need to take myself off to a room by myself and try to alleviate the feeling as much as I can by doing the hair gripping. I also get urges to scratch my wrists until they bleed (sometimes I do this during the night when I'm particularly stressed and don't even realise I've done it until the next morning) or to obsessively pick the skin around my fingers, but usually the hair gripping does the trick. Michael finds it very distressing to watch, which is why I go somewhere on my own. After 10 minutes or so, I usually start to calm down and am able to carry on with life.

The doctor that morning was lovely with me, even though I had never been seen by her before. I think sometimes one of the hardest things for someone with an ongoing mental health issue to deal with is the fact that there is no continuity of care; I could see any one of half a dozen different doctors at my surgery and patients can't usually specify who they would prefer to see – it's just pot-luck. But luckily the doctor who dealt with me that day was very understanding and actually gave me a new perspective on my illness.

'Sometimes,' she explained to Mum, who always tries to look for a rational reason as to why things happen, 'there is no reason. Sometimes it can be as simple as waking up one morning and feeling like the world has collapsed all around you. There might not be anything specific that's triggered this, it just happens.'

But, in this instance, we did know why it was happening. It was the result of me coming off my medication with no medical consultation. When my illness is at its worst, as it was that day, I find it hard to even look at anybody. I become almost childlike, unable to take care of myself, and I am lucky that I have lots of people that will step in and look after me in that situation. I'm sure some people are not so fortunate. I sat there looking at my hands, trying to string sentences together that would not formulate. In the end, I managed to articulate that I didn't want to be on the medication anymore. I just wanted to be normal again.

'I have patients,' the doctor began, 'who will need to be on medication for the rest of their lives. And if taking a tablet every day allows them to live a relatively normal life, then there's no problem with that.'

Even through the haze of my illness, I saw that she was right.

I was initially signed off work for two weeks and started to take my Clomipramine again that same day. The next morning, Mum and I took Jacob for his two-year check with the health visitor. Even though the health visitor was very pleased with Jacob's general health, she was very critical of his use of a dummy. I had already been feeling incredibly guilty about this in recent months and was trying to wean him off. I knew very well that dummy-use could affect Jacob's talking and his teeth, but I like to think that I'm a fairly intelligent person and was constantly monitoring his usage, making sure he was only having it at sleep times and making sure he had regular dental check-ups. In short, I was doing the best I could while also trying to preserve my own mental health.

I think that, sometimes, more focus needs to be put onto what parents are doing well rather than looking for a reason to criticise us, even if it is done with the best of intentions. For someone who is not feeling at all mentally strong, any criticism, no matter how small, can seem like a massive blow and a huge slight on their parenting. Personally, I began to worry once again that the health visitor would report me, and that Jacob would be taken away from us – not only because he was still using a dummy, but also because I know I came across as spaced out and "strange" in that meeting. Mum was in there with me and I let her do most of the talking. I imagine the health visitor must have thought me incapable of taking care of a toddler, but I'll never know. I wish our health services were so much more joined up than they are; if only the health visitor could have been informed of my difficulties beforehand, maybe she would have adjusted her words and manner accordingly. She had no idea I'd seen the doctor just the day before and was in the middle of a crisis.

*

Jacob and I stayed with Mum and Dad for a few days after that until I started to feel stronger, which allowed Michael to be able to return to work. He works as a security officer and is not salaried, so he needs to be there to get paid – something that would have been extremely difficult when my issues first arose if my parents hadn't been there for us. I will always be grateful to them – we both will.

After a week, I began to feel a little stronger. My line manager came out with her line manager to see me at home. Prior to this, I had only ever really mentioned my issues in passing at work, as I had been terrified that I would be deemed unsuitable to do my job. I need to work to have a purpose to my life; without it, my mental health would start to decline again.

By the time the two of them arrived at the house, I had settled it in my mind that I was going to be completely open and honest about my issues. I felt I owed it to them and to myself. After all, how could they help if they didn't know the full story? So that's what I did. Starting from the beginning, with the fertility problems, the failed adoption, the pregnancy and birth, and beyond. I told them about my hospital admission, my big meltdown, my diagnosis, and the delicate balance that was still going on with my medication.

I could tell that some things were starting to make sense to them as I was talking, such as the way my speech has become much slower since taking the Clomipramine and the way I struggle to find the right words sometimes. They must have been wondering why this was suddenly the case when I had been fine before going off on maternity leave!

We talked at length about how I could be best supported at work. All I needed was the knowledge that people now knew and would understand if I sometimes acted differently to how I normally am. It was like a huge weight had been lifted; just knowing that people would know was enough, and I was able to return happily to work the following week. Now, if I need time alone or just need to get away from my desk for a few minutes, I have the support there that I need. I have never worked anywhere like it before, where every colleague is a friend.

My relationships with my family have changed for the better too. Before my diagnosis, there was little understanding of mental health conditions within the family, and I include myself in that. There is no history of mental illness on either of my parents' sides of the family, so we all learnt together how to deal with it and the dos and don'ts. Towards the beginning of my illness, before my diagnosis, Mum actually said to me, 'Well, everyone has a bit of anxiety.'

She wasn't trying to patronise me or make light of the situation; I just believe she genuinely did not understand the difference between being a bit of a worrier and having a full-blown illness. I suppose it was a bit like saying, 'Well, everyone's arms ache sometimes,' to somebody with a broken wrist, but it made complete sense to her at that time.

I felt so frustrated by her comment, even though there was no negativity intended. If my own mum was saying this, how could the rest of the world begin to understand what it's like for those of us who are suffering? I think that's a major reason why many people still try to hide their illnesses away, because the perception still exists that if it's not something you can see or touch, then it's not really there. I like to think that my family and I have been educated together and that we have educated each other in a way too. It has been through seeing their distress during my worst times that I've learnt how much of an affect an illness like mine can have on others. Michael has admitted that he sometimes worries about saying the wrong thing to me in case it sets off an episode. And I hate that. All I want is to be treated the same as everybody else. (It's still a work in progress.)

The day of my meltdown, the doctor also referred me for assessment for a talking therapy. I was seen very quickly with the local NHS Wellbeing Service. My assessment appointment came through very quickly and I was ultimately referred on to a course of cognitive behavioural therapy, which I would attend once a week. My therapist discussed at length with me what I hoped to achieve through the CBT, which really helped to clarify everything in my mind.

'More than anything, I want to stop catastrophising as soon as I have a rotten night's sleep,' I told her. 'I want to sleep normally again.'

Together, we came up with a plan to help with this. I started to keep a prompt sheet next to my bed and, as soon as I started to feel that all-too-familiar sense of dread and doom when I couldn't get to sleep straightaway, I would look at the sheet and it would take me, step-by-step, through what to do. This included a breathing plan (when I'm in the height of my panic, I completely forget to breathe) and a way to rein in my thoughts before they took over me completely. I wasn't going to die, I could still be a good mum if I was tired, and I could still do my job if I was tired.

For me, one of the main benefits of CBT was that I was able to determine my own aims and the methods of achieving those aims, rather than being told what to do. Being quite a methodical person, I appreciated the way my therapist helped me to break my issues down and learn to deal with them one at a time, rather than seeing them as one large ball of emotions that's impossible to manage as a whole.

I see my course of CBT as a wholly positive experience; it is yet another tool in my mental health first-aid kit that I can call upon when I need it. As time goes on, I begin to feel as though I'm slowly becoming an expert on my own condition and how to deal with it. But, just like with a physical illness, there will always be more to learn as my illness changes and evolves.

CHAPTER 26

Reflections

Whenever I pause now to take stock of how my life has changed over the last six years, I can scarcely believe that all of those things happened to me and not to somebody else. Parts of my story read to me now like the script from a soap opera – the failed adoption and the pregnancy, for example. And if it were a soap opera, I'd have been the first to say, 'That would never happen. Finding out you're pregnant two days after adopting twins? Never.'

But it did happen, and it could again. I'm not saying that anyone else will ever go through the exact same things that we did at the same times, but parts of it can and will happen again. And I want, more than anything, for no one else to ever feel as alone as I did. Please know that your own story is valid and any thoughts you may be having will have been had by someone else at some point in time, I guarantee you.

I would like all new parents to know that the expectations you have of yourselves, most likely because you think the world has these expectations of you too, are unrealistic. You have not failed if you don't get out of the house until lunchtime. You will *not* harm your baby by formula-feeding. You might well not brush your hair for two days running. This is normal. We are all different and our babies are all different, so why try to compare ourselves with others? Actually, I can't answer that because I did it, and I still do it now sometimes. But guess what? That's normal too!

Well-meaning people in your life will try to get you to go out with your baby as much as possible, and of course, it is important to have a change of scene and some adult conversation – but do it at your own pace. If you're struggling one day, leave it and try again the next day. It's hard when you are still feeling so vulnerable and fragile from giving birth, but please don't let others dictate what is right for you. Trust your own instincts.

Please don't feel like a freak, like I did, if you don't feel that rush of love for your baby from day one that everyone else seems to. Again, we are all different and we all build relationships in different ways; why would it be any different with your baby? Some loves are slow-burners, but does this make them any less valid? No. For me, it only made the love I started to feel for Jacob, all those months after his birth, shine all the brighter.

Close your ears when others tell you about how well their baby is sleeping or how they can roll over three times, forward roll onto the yoga mat and end with a back-flip at four months old. Smile politely and nod. That's all you can do. Then secretly have a laugh about it later. Yes, you are a parent, but you're also still you, and you don't need to suddenly become a different person just because you have a baby. Parent in the way you feel comfortable and don't try to be someone else's ideal of what a parent should be. Because trust me, it won't work and will just make you miserable. And if you're miserable, so is your baby.

In terms of my own illness, in a broad sense, I was initially diagnosed under the umbrella term of postnatal depression, although I never use this phrase myself as I feel it is misleading in my case. There are some people for whom it is a perfect descriptor of their illness, but not for everyone, and not for me. Postnatal mental illness is about so much more than depression. I tend to say that I suffered "perinatal mental health issues" rather than "postnatal depression". The term "perinatal" covers everything from pregnancy up until the baby turns one, and I never actually had "classic" depression, so I feel mental health issues is a better descriptor for me. And now, four years on from the onset of my illness, I can no longer be classed as perinatal, so now I just tell people that I have various mental health issues that were initially triggered during pregnancy.

My insomnia is stable for the moment; I am generally sleeping well and use my Zopiclone as a crutch when I need it, probably about once a month on average. But I am still very aware of it and know that I'll always have to monitor my sleep carefully and be conscious of possibly becoming obsessed with it. There's a certain irony in that – I have to try so hard not to obsess over the subject of sleep, while still being hyper-aware of my own relationship with it.

Sleep isn't the only thing I obsess over, however; I sometimes become obsessive over other things too, and Michael usually has to tell me when I'm doing it so that I can try to rein it in. For example, if I have lots of little things on my mind and lots of things that need doing, I meticulously write detailed lists and become obsessed with ticking things off once they're done. If I don't manage to get them done when I was expecting to, I then become very heightened and anxious, talking about it non-stop in a really fast, high-pitched voice. I can't sit down, can't concentrate on anything else.

'You don't know you're doing it,' Michael tells me. 'You start off by just mentioning whatever it is that you need to do, and then I notice that this intensifies, and you become more and more fixated on it. You can't think about anything else.'

I'm also battling with my body image. During my pregnancy, I had made my peace with the fact that my body was going to change dramatically and I didn't mind; I could accept it as it was inevitable. I even enjoyed the freedom of it, and ate whatever I liked, putting almost four stone on in the process. What I hadn't been prepared for, however, was that my body wasn't just going to snap back into place once the baby was born.

Throughout the pregnancy I heard comments such as, 'You'll be back in your regular jeans the day after the birth, like I was' or 'You're naturally slim, so you'll have no trouble getting back to a size eight.'

Perhaps if I'd had my baby 10 years earlier, this might have been true. But in fact, I remained two and a half stone heavier than my pre-pregnancy weight after having Jacob, and I couldn't deal with it. I felt like I was not in control of my body anymore. I felt hideous and unattractive – I still do a lot of the time.

Indeed, three years on from my diagnosis, I still have my bad days. The forgetfulness has been the hardest side effect of my medicine to deal with. As well as my short-term memory being affected (long-term is fine), I will often have blanks in terms of what I am trying to say and the words I want to use evade me. Then as soon as I start to focus on it, it gets even worse and my whole brain feels like it has shut down. This makes me feel very self-conscious, especially in the work setting when I need to come across as professional and credible. I feel very embarrassed about it sometimes, especially if people try to finish my sentences for me. I then torture myself by remembering what it was I was trying to say as soon as they have left, and feel like I want to kick myself. It makes me feel stupid when I use completely the wrong word in the wrong context, which happens daily.

Being medicated isn't an automatic cure for all those dark thoughts, and that's okay. I've started to come to terms with that now. My illness will always be with me, but it is no longer bigger than me. Mostly, I am in control of it rather than it being in control of me. Some days, however, I do get overwhelmed by my thoughts and obsessions and will simply tell those around me what's happening so that they don't expect more of me than I can give. Thankfully, I can go for weeks or months without having such a day now, so it's a part of me and my life, rather than being the ruler of my world.

Depression is a fairly new string to my mental health bow, beginning for me in November 2018. One weekend I just felt really down and couldn't stop crying but I didn't know why. I felt like a huge weight had settled on my chest and was bearing down, suffocating me. I felt so frightened, as though I just wanted to bolt out of the house and drive away and never stop, or run and run and never look back. I didn't know what was happening to me, so I went back to my GP, who confirmed it sounded more like depression than any of my existing issues and referred me back to the wellbeing service.

I am now embarking on another course of CBT and counselling, since I believe there is still more to explore in terms of my feelings about the adoption. I still think of the twins every day and I know Michael does too. The pain of that situation doesn't go away, but sometimes, very occasionally, I can think of them now without feeling those deep, dark feelings of shame. It's as though, with the benefit of time, I have started to reframe that whole situation in my head. I say "started to" because it is still a work in progress and I know that I might never be able to do so completely, but at least now I can look back on that time with some sense of reality, knowing that what happened was dark and terrible, but that it happened for a valid reason and not because I am a monster.

I know we made the only decision we could have at the time, but sometimes my mind likes to torment me with thoughts that we might have done the wrong thing. I see them sometimes, in my mind's eye, playing on the swings in the park or laughing with their friends at school, and I am grateful to have known them for even that brief time. They will always be a part of our story, and us a part of theirs. I hope they are happy and loved and fabulous. There are parts of the Snow Patrol song 'You Could be Happy' that remind me of them so much.

'You could be happy and I won't know. But you weren't happy the day I watched you go. / You could be happy; I hope you are. You made me happier than I'd been by far. / Do the things that you always wanted to, without me there to hold you back; don't think, just do.'

While I'm scared as hell to revisit this again, I understand and accept that it's going to be a necessary part of my ongoing recovery.

On the days where my illness *does* rear its ugly head, it feels like dark skies are closing in around me, smothering me, and I'm unable to focus or order my thoughts properly. I become so tense that I forget to breathe properly and often have to be reminded to take a breath. I feel a sense of doom and just want to hide away from everyone. I struggle to form coherent sentences and can't find the right words. I suppose to anyone who doesn't know me, it looks bad, really bad. But to me, my worst days now are better than even the best days I had before my diagnosis, and to me that feels like a win. I am still here, I am no longer wishing myself dead, and I no longer think my illness is going to kill me. I suppose what I'm trying to say is that, with the right support around me, I have learnt to cope, which can only be a positive.

Being honest with people has helped my recovery so much. It means that I don't internalise things as much and that it's not such a big deal if I need to ask for help or if I need to remove myself from a certain situation, because people are already aware of why I might need to do that.

At first, I worried that telling people might make them treat me differently than before, but I haven't found this to be the case at all. The media definitely perpetuates some of the myths around mental illness to help reinforce those dated stereotypes of "nut-jobs" or "headcases", but, in real life, I've found that these stereotypes aren't actually carried by most people. If anything, the stigma perpetuated in the media is outdated now, and people see through it. Most people listen to me, acknowledge my illness as they would a physical one, and then are generally happy to move on to another topic of conversation. And this is what I want. I wanted to be treated normally, but at the same time I'm happy to be open about it and will merrily bore anyone senseless talking about my issues if they are curious.

My friend Nicole recently told me, 'There are still times now that I worry you are struggling but it's very difficult to ask outright and I think all of us find that the same.'

My reply was simple: just ask me outright. That goes for anyone. I'll always be honest and it might be that there's nothing anyone can do to change how I'm feeling, but just chatting about it helps so much.

As my life continues to move forward and Jacob gets older, I am determined to fulfil my life's ambition to write full-time. In a strange way, I am grateful for my illness as it has given me the platform to be able to publish my story and thus start me on the road to achieving this goal. I also want to continue to advocate for women (and men) who cannot find their voice and are lost in the haze of their mental illness, and I will always be grateful to Trigger and The Shaw Mind Foundation for giving me the precious gift of that opportunity.

I am positive about the future. Remarkably, we have just found out that Jacob is going to be a big brother later this year, something that we never thought would be possible. As if one miracle wasn't enough, we're now being blessed twice over! I feel happy but cautious, and am already taking steps to protect my mental health as the pregnancy progresses. I know that there's a good chance I'll need to formula-feed again so that I can allow Michael to help out with feeds during the night while the baby is still feeding regularly. And you know what? I've made my peace with that this time around. It's not ideal, no, but if it's what I need to do to keep myself well and be a good mum, so be it.

I feel like the path I've travelled has helped me to find out more about myself than I ever knew before. I know now that I need routine, familiarity, and sleep! I know that being a stay-at-home mum was not good for my mental health. And I have learnt, after years of being quiet and shy, never wanting to rock the boat, how to be assertive and stand up for myself.

Just the other day, one of my friends at work commented on the huge change in me since becoming a mum. 'You're like a different person. So confident and in control. I noticed the difference in you as soon as you came back to work.' I think that part of this comes from having to advocate for myself and Jacob, sometimes having to fight to access services or medication. I had to get stronger, and quickly. I feel this change too – now I will say straight out if I'm unhappy about anything or think something is wrong. And I'm hoping this will mean I'm a stronger mum to Jacob as he grows up too, willing to speak up on his behalf and teaching him to do the same whenever he sees an injustice.

I feel as though I'm more positive than I was before; I've been to hell, seen what it looks like, and come back again. And I never want to go there again.

But, overall, I treasure the little things that make me happy now; a certain song, the changing of the seasons, someone taking the time to make me smile.

I appreciate so many things about my life now that I took for granted before. My relationships with my family and friends have survived the ultimate test and are stronger because of it.

Michael is still (and always will be) the anchor that grounds me when I need to be grounded and calms me when I need to be calmed. He's still here despite everything we've been through. That can only make me love him in more ways than I loved him before.

And as for Jacob? Our relationship changes and evolves every day. I have never loved or been loved so unconditionally and I truly believe that the adversity we both faced in the early part of his life has played its part in that. I know that the day will come that he will want to read his mum's book, and, Jacob, if you have made it this far, my darling, I hope you can understand that the difficulties we had were because of your mum's illness and not because I didn't love you. I have always loved you; it just took me a little longer than usual to uncover that love because the things happening inside my brain conspired to conceal it. I am so fortunate to be your mum. I adore you and am proud of you every single day. I hope you don't feel that I've compromised your privacy by talking about you and us so openly; the truth is that I would never have had a story to tell in the first place without you, because you are and always will be the biggest part of me. I am grateful for this story that we have written together because it has only made me cherish every little thing about you even more.

For any parents reading this who may be struggling, please know that things will be okay again at some point in the future. It's so hard to hold on to that thought when you're in the thick of it, I know, but there is help out there. Even if you have to fight for it sometimes, even if you're made to feel like there's nothing wrong because you're putting on a good show for the world and have had the audacity to brush your hair and put on a bit of make-up and some people can't see past that, please keep knocking on those doors. And when it gets too much, rope in everyone around you to help. They will want to support you – just imagine if the roles were reversed. Be kind to yourself and don't expect too much too soon. You deserve to be helped and one day you will be able to see that.

When the wind blows, of course the cradle is going to rock. The trick is to recognise it before the bough breaks completely.

PLAYLIST

Music has played – and continues to play – a huge part in my story. At various times throughout the past four years, I can remember with a certain clarity the songs that were playing in the background when particular things were happening. At other times, I have used music to help me make sense of what I was going through, or to elicit a particular emotion that I needed to feel at that time. This was especially important because my medication, like that of countless others with mental health issues, often dulls my reaction to what is happening. I might need to feel a certain way in order to bring my feelings to the fore and to ensure I'm not bottling things up, but my medication doesn't always allow this, so I sometimes use music to help trigger whatever feeling it is that I need to feel in order to come to terms with what is happening.

'Fix You' – Coldplay

'This Woman's Work' – Heather Bush

'74, 75' – The Connells

'Linger' – The Cranberries

'You Can't Always Get What You Want' – The Rolling Stones

'A Whiter Shade of Pale' – Procol Harum

'Everybody Hurts' – REM

'Every You Every Me' – Placebo

'Itchycoo Park' – The Small Faces

'You Could be Happy' – Snow Patrol

ACKNOWLEDGEMENTS

I have to start by thanking Michael for always giving me the time to write and edit. All those trips to the soft-play gave me the space to be able to do justice to my story, and I will never be able to thank you enough.

Thank you to Jen, Amanda and Heather for letting me use your quotes.

And thank you to Stephanie and Katie, my wonderful editors at Trigger, for not always agreeing with me and for never minding me having strong opinions on things. You have been more patient than I have deserved.

Author Q&A

Ali Sanders

1. How are you feeling about finishing your book?

Exhausted, happy and proud. There were times I thought I'd never get to the end of it – there was so much I wanted to say, and it seemed impossible to fit everything in, but I got there with the help of my fabulous editors and the support of my family and friends.

2. Tell us about the writing process! What was your favourite part?

I think my favourite part was right at the beginning, when I was planning what was going to be included. I found it so therapeutic to just spill everything out onto the pages and I didn't worry about the logistics of getting it in an order that made sense until later on. I also really enjoyed writing about the younger years with my friends. Some of those memories made me cry with laughter!

3. What was the hardest part?

For me, the hardest part was definitely the chapters where I talk about the twins. I left these parts until quite late, late on in the process because I still find the details quite painful to go over. But I knew from the start that if I was going to tell my story, I needed to tell it all.

4. Did you have any routines that helped you to write?

As somebody who works full-time and also has a very energetic toddler to look after, I didn't have the luxury of being able to just write as and when the mood took me. I had to be quite disciplined and set chunks of time aside during the evenings and weekends when I could fit in an hour or two. Michael was amazing at giving me child-free time so I could concentrate!

5. Do you have any tips for other people who might be thinking about writing their own memoir?

My top tip would be to do what I did initially, and write it just for yourself. That way, I didn't feel as though I needed to hold back on anything because I wasn't intending for anyone else to read it. If it goes all the way to publication, what a fantastic bonus!

6. What does Michael think of you writing your story?

He feels it has been great for my mental wellbeing and that it has helped us to be more open about my issues as a couple. He says he is also unbelievably proud and hopes it helps the conversation around mental health – even if it only helps one person, then it's been worthwhile.

7. What do you hope your readers take away from this book?

Lots of things. Hopefully a newfound respect for adopters and foster carers, who really are the most incredible people. I hope it will make people think twice before quizzing others about their plans for a family. I hope it will open people's eyes up to how different and varied the symptoms of perinatal depression can be, rather than only being "classic" depression. Most of all, I hope that someone, somewhere, might relate in even a tiny way to my experiences so that they don't have to feel as alone as I did.

8. What's your next project?

There is definitely some fiction on the horizon – my creative sensors are well and truly tingling! I am constantly writing short stories and poetry, but I would like to have a go at my first novel now. And, of course, lots of mental health advocacy.

9. What would you say to someone who relates to your story?

Please don't feel alone. You're not a freak, and you can get better and enjoy life again, no matter how impossible it feels right now. Yes, your mental illness will always be with you, but with the right help, there will come a time when it will just be a facet of you rather than everything you are. Do whatever you need to do to get that help, even if you feel you're not strong enough. That first step is the toughest.

10. What advice do you have for someone whose loved one is suffering from PPD?

Try and understand as much as you can about their individual illness; everyone is so different and the things we need to be able to start getting better are many and varied. For me, it was some child-free time with friends that got the ball rolling. Anything you can do to try and make your loved one feel a bit like their old self will help.

11. How are you feeling about the future?

Nervous, excited, a little bit terrified, but very, very happy.

12. If you could sum up your story in three words, what would they be?

Unbelievable, intense, and wonderful.

If you found this book interesting ... why not read these next?

Postpartum Depression and Anxiety

The Definitive Survival and Recovery Approach

A refreshing, compassionate and user-friendly self-help book to guide and support parents experiencing postpartum depression and anxiety.

Daddy Blues

Postnatal Depression and Fatherhood

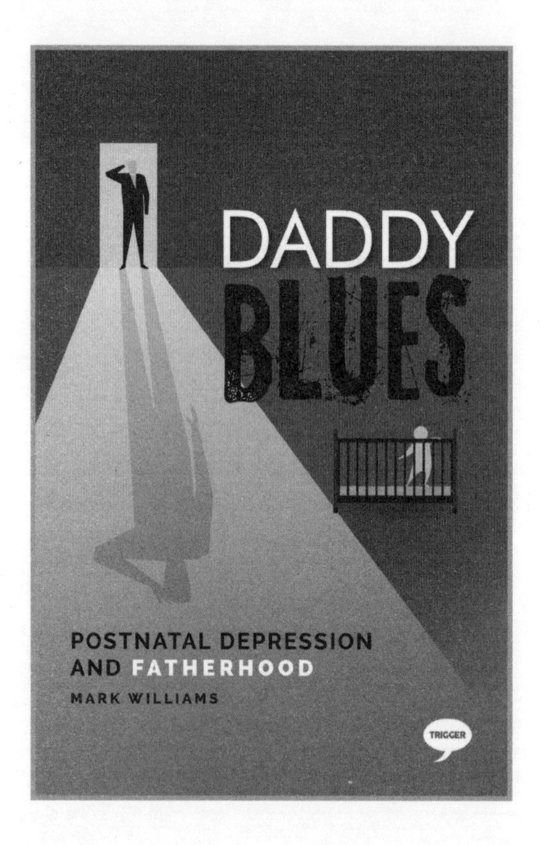

Mark knew of baby blues for mothers, but never thought it might happen to him. And then it did. *Daddy Blues* explores a story we all know, from a different perspective.

Rattled

Overcoming Postpartum Psychosis

When Jen Wight gave birth to her son, she thought it was all uphill from there. But she was wrong. *Rattled* is the story of her journey through psychosis.

EXTRACT FROM RATTLED

CHAPTER 9

DON'T YOU KNOW I'M LOCO?

Dr Martin Luther King said, 'I have a dream', and then he woke up.

My diary entry.

The psychosis starts with Renée Zellweger.

Before the baby's arrival, I had a chat with one of our neighbours. Emily is a lovely lady in her sixties with a silver bob and bright eyes. She's from England and swims in the sea every day no matter what the weather. As we chatted, both folding our respective washing from the line, she told me that her daughter – whose child was due around the same time as ours – is coming over from LA to stay with her.

'How wonderful,' I said.

'She's an actor.'

'Really cool.'

This fact lodged itself deep in my brain.

It is now Monday of week six, and as we are leaving the apartment, I see a woman clutching a very small baby. *Ah*, I think, *that must be Emily's daughter*. Her face looks very familiar.

That morning we have the six-week check for mother and baby with Dr Harper. Kai is going in to work late so he can come with me. While waiting in the reception I flick through a copy of Grazia and see a photo of a woman clutching a small baby. It looks exactly like Emily's daughter. I check the name by the picture. Renée Zellweger.

It isn't a very flattering shot; she's wearing thick-rimmed glasses and her already-small eyes are squinted into raisins in her round pale face. It is also quite blurry like it was shot from a distance and the photo editor had magnified it many times.

'Oh, my God,' I say to Kai. 'I think Renée Zellweger is in our building. She's Emily's daughter.'

'I don't think so, Jen,' says Kai. 'Are you feeling okay?'

'Yes, sure – I'm just so happy.'

I carry on flicking through the magazine and hit on another photo which stops me in my tracks.

'Look – it's Howard!'

I wave the magazine at Kai. The photo shows the new mystery man in Sandra Bullock's life. He looks exactly like a crazy party-hound called Howard, an old college friend of Kai's.

'That isn't Howard.'

'Yes, it is.'

'It isn't, Jen. I know Howard and that isn't him.'

'But it looks exactly like him – and he knows famous people, doesn't he?'

'He does, yes. But that's not him.'

He turns back to his iPhone to check his work emails. I know it's Howard; Kai just isn't looking properly. *He works too hard*. I turn the page of the magazine and see a photo of Halle Berry – but wait, that looks just like my friend Gina! I stare at the photo. I haven't seen Gina in a while; maybe she's secretly living a double life in Tufnell Park when she's not in LA ... Then I see a picture of Lindsay Lohan and it is our friend Clare, who's married to Kai's old uni friend, Peter.

The magazine is transformed from a glossy gossip mag into an item of extreme importance. It seems to glow with secret knowledge in my hands. I turn the next page as though I'm in the British Library handling Shakespeare's *First Folio* with white-gloved hands. *How do I know all these famous people? This seems so odd*. Then a thought occurs to me. *Maybe I'm famous too*.

I look around the waiting room and feel a great upwelling of happiness. I am beaming. I catch the eye of a mother, sitting opposite me with her child. She gives me a brief smile then looks away, embarrassed. I notice one of the receptionists glancing at me, too.

Why is everyone acting so weirdly towards me? I wonder. I turn another page of the magazine and see a picture of Cameron Diaz. And she looks exactly like me.

Oh, my God, I'm Cameron Diaz.

I look at Kai and he smiles back at me. In the picture, Cameron is wearing the blue shirt and cut-off shorts that I wear all the time. *I must have come to Australia, like Renée, to get away from the paparazzi while we have our baby.*

I look at Kai again and think, *the lucky bastard, he gets to have sex with Cameron Diaz / Me.*

I am tallish, and was slim before the baby came. I like surfing. I have blonde hair and I love dancing. These things prove I must be Cameron Diaz. (My addled brain is conveniently ignoring the things we don't have in common, like me not being a world-famous movie star who once went out with Justin Timberlake.)

You may think this doesn't make sense – surely I must know I'm not Cameron Diaz? But I don't and here's why. I think I'm Cameron Diaz, which is quite a mad thing to think, so I'm either mad or I'm Cameron Diaz. I know I'm not mad; I survived the horrendous night in the hospital. Therefore, I *must* be Cameron Diaz. You see? At the time, it seemed like a simple mathematical equation.

'The doctor is ready for you now,' says the receptionist, and I carefully put the precious magazine down. I am blazing with happiness and a bit wobbly on my feet, as you might expect you would be after discovering you're a world-famous actress who has secretly moved to Australia to have a baby with her "civilian" husband.

'How are you doing, Jen?' asks the doctor.

I flash him a knowing smile. *So, we're all just going to go along with my alias. That's fine by me.*

'Well, my scar is still weeping a bit and sore in parts, but other than that I'm fine. I'm really happy actually.'

He smiles at me and Kai.

'Let me take a look.'

I hop up onto the couch, lift my dress and roll down the top of my knickers.

'How is the little one?' he asks as he bends over my nether regions.

'He is a little angel, really – the perfect baby.'

My son gurgles in the buggy as if in agreement.

Dr Harper looks at me and raises his eyebrows. I imagine new mums aren't usually filled with such unbridled enthusiasm at week six. But then, not many new mums have come to the startling realisation that they are one of the most beautiful women in the world.

'Good. Then let's have a look here.' Dr Harper pauses and frowns, bending further over me to get a closer look. 'I think I know why your scar isn't healing properly. They've left part of the stitch material in.'

'Oh,' I say, a million miles away thinking about my jet-set lifestyle in Hollywood, and what I'm going to do next in my career.

'I'm really sorry about this, Jen. I'll be having stern words with the hospital.'

'That's okay; everyone makes mistakes sometimes.'

'You'll need to take a course of antibiotics.'

'No problems.'

He reaches for some metal pincers and sets about pulling out what looks like a very manky piece of blue string. It breaks open two of the scabs, which start to bleed again. He presses a pad of white cotton-wool dressing to the wound.

'There, that should do it, Jen.'

He helps me to my feet and I rearrange my dress. *Should I just say it? We are safe here in his little office; no one is going to know if I just come out with it ...*

I laugh and give him a wink. 'I can't thank you enough for everything you've done. I'm so happy!'

My famous megawatt smile almost blinds him. I bet it's pretty unnerving having such a famous patient.

We are clustered at the door of his office in an awkward bundle. He reaches his hand out, but I go for his cheek instead and he laughs. I imagine him telling his wife, 'Cameron Diaz kissed me today', and them both laughing over it.

'You do seem very happy,' he agrees as he shakes Kai's hand.

As we head down in the lift, I give Kai a massive hug. I can see us reflected in the polished metal of the lift wall and I stare in disbelief. I don't see Cameron Diaz's face staring back at me. It is just plain old Jen.

'I'm not Cameron Diaz, am I?' I ask.

Kai pulls out of the hug and looks me hard in the face.

'Are you sure you're okay?'

I laugh. 'Yeah.'

He frowns at me and I smile back at him.

'What do you mean then?'

'Oh nothing,' I say. 'Just a thought.'

the Shaw mind
FOUNDATION
Creating hope for children,
adults and families

www.triggerpublishing.com

Trigger is a publishing house devoted to opening conversations about mental health. We tell the stories of people who have suffered from mental illnesses and recovered, so that others may learn from them.

Adam Shaw is a worldwide mental health advocate and philanthropist. Now in recovery from mental health issues, he is committed to helping others suffering from debilitating mental health issues through the global charity he co-founded, The Shaw Mind Foundation. www.shawmindfoundation.org

Lauren Callaghan (CPsychol, PGDipClinPsych, PgCert, MA (hons), LLB (hons), BA), born and educated in New Zealand, is an innovative industry-leading psychologist based in London, United Kingdom. Lauren has worked with children and young people, and their families, in a number of clinical settings providing evidence based treatments for a range of illnesses, including anxiety and obsessional problems. She was a psychologist at the specialist national treatment centres for severe obsessional problems in the UK and is renowned as an expert in the field of mental health, recognised for diagnosing and successfully treating OCD and anxiety related illnesses in particular. In addition to appearing as a treating clinician in the critically acclaimed and BAFTA award-winning documentary *Bedlam*, Lauren is a frequent guest speaker on mental health conditions in the media and at academic conferences. Lauren also acts as a guest lecturer and honorary researcher at the Institute of Psychiatry Kings College, UCL.